# NARRATIVE DISCOURSE ANALYSIS FOR TEACHER EDUCATORS

## *Managing Cultural Differences in Classrooms*

**Discourse and Social Processes**
**Lesley A. Rex, series editor**

# NARRATIVE DISCOURSE ANALYSIS FOR TEACHER EDUCATORS

## Managing Cultural Differences in Classrooms

*edited by*

Lesley Rex
*University of Michigan*

Mary M. Juzwik
*Michigan State University*

HAMPTON PRESS, INC.
NEW YORK, NEW YORK

Printed in the United States of America

Library of Congress Cataloging-in-Publication Data

Narrative discourse analysis for teacher educators : managing cultural difference in classrooms / edited by Lesley Rex and Mary Juzwik
     p. cm. -- (Discourse and social processes)
    Includes bibliographical references and index.
    ISBN 978-1-61289-044-9 (hbk.) -- ISBN 978-1-61289-045-6 (pbk.)
  1. Interaction analysis in education. 2. Discourse analysis, Narrative.
3. Multicultural education. I. Rex, Lesley A. II. Juzwik, Mary M. (Mary Margaret)
   LB1034.N37 2011
   307.117--dc23
                  2011024397

Hampton Press, Inc.
307 Seventh Avenue
New York, NY 10001

# Contents

# Acknowledgments and Dedication

This book project began as a symposium, titled *Narrative Research and Literacy Teacher Education*, conducted at the annual meeting of the American Educational Research Association meeting in Montreal in 2005. We are grateful to Laura Roop, Joanne Larson, and Mary Catherine O'Connor, who reviewed earlier drafts of the manuscript and provided detailed and helpful feedback. We thank Staci Schultz for her assistance with editing, proofing, and organizing the chapters. We also appreciate Hsuan-Yi Huang's indexing help.

Mary would like to thank Matt Ferkany for his intellectual companionship, kindness, and support throughout the project. She dedicates this book to Margaret and Stephen Juzwik, her first significant narrators and teachers. Lesley dedicates this book with loving appreciation to Brian Taggart in recognition of his enduring patience while she works.

# 1

## INTRODUCTION
## Narrative Discourse Analysis
## for Teacher Educators:
## Considering Participation, Difference, and Ethics

*Lesley A. Rex*

Productive discussions are difficult, especially about tough topics. As teacher educators, we all want to build with our students open-minded stances that engender critical inquiry, Socratic dialogues, and socially just advocacy. We find ourselves continually facing down the communal urge to avoid tension and the individual drive to escape vulnerability. As devil's advocates, for example, we prompt pre-service and in-service teachers to resist their own and their students' desire to belong and feel comfortable. We encourage them to assert themselves and to trouble the water in pursuit of greater understanding for themselves and their students. Some, especially those who live as social outsiders and experience the continual disenfranchisement of their position, are only too happy to do so, while too many adopt the rhetoric of cultural diversity without putting themselves out there. When meaningful conversations finally catalyze, the intense attention they require saps everyone's energies in large part because engaging in self-protection and social relationship while tackling formidable issues is exhausting work. This book is based on the premise that, as difficult and tiring as this work can be for new and experienced teachers, generating extended discussions of provocative, change-making issues while promoting respectful social cohesion in classrooms and professional relationships is key to success and satisfaction. Theirs as well as ours.

We university-based authors in this volume occupy the roles of teacher, teacher educator, and education researcher. In addition to teaching in universities, we have taught in public elementary and secondary schools; and as teacher educators, we are regularly involved with pre- and in-service teachers. As education researchers, we utilize linguistic and discourse analytic methods to explore the complications of classroom teaching and learning, principally in literacy classrooms. For this project, we foreground our role as teacher educators and draw from our teacher education experience, as well as from our research, to focus on three interrelated pedagogical areas teacher educators navigate to involve students in productive classroom dialogues: participation, difference, and ethics. We are continually faced with decisions about how to invite and maintain student participation, how to make positive use of cultural differences, and how to evaluate the ethics of our decisions. Our goal in this book is to help teacher educators deal more effectively with these three pedagogical issues by understanding the narratives we and our pre- and in-service teachers tell during stressful conversations involving cultural difference.

## TENSIONS AS SITES FOR DIALOGUE AND LEARNING

As a long-time teacher educator, I know only too well how demanding tense exchanges are, and that managing one doesn't necessarily mean the next one will be any easier. I also know that each one teaches me something useful. I've chosen three to demonstrate what I mean and to introduce this book. As you'll see, I have not chosen moments when I appear heroic or even successful in my teaching. If I'd had the benefit of hindsight at the time, I would have made different discursive choices, which is the reason for providing the examples. They convey the high stakes and uncomfortable tensions generated by these kinds of conversations, as well as my post hoc reflections.

In the first case, I was working with experienced teachers who were well practiced in taking on difficult issues, when they chose to do so. The exchange that follows occurred when Monica, the spokesperson for our English teacher professional study group, called for a meeting. She was concerned about something I announced at the previous session and had surveyed the other teachers in the group before coming to me. This was the first time in the group's 8-year existence that I, the organizer of the group, had been so formally called to task. The feeling around the table was tense, as five other teacher leaders listened to our exchange.

> Monica:   You said that you thought it was time to focus on issues
>           related to race, and that bothered me. You didn't consult
>           with us first. You just made that decision.

> Lesley:   I thought that it was time since we hadn't focused on those issues yet, and that doing so could help us think about what complicates your practice.
>
> Monica: That's not what we are here for. Race isn't the issue. And it would stir up things we don't need to stir up.

Like me, Monica, an English department chair, is white.[1] The teachers in the three high school study groups are evenly split between white and black, and 95% of their students are black. Monica was right on all counts. For the 8 years the group studied how to improve their reading and writing curriculum and instruction, no one had broached how race might be involved in their practice. Aware that it was a "touchy" subject, I too had avoided raising the issue, waiting until one of the teachers did. I had been avoiding and waiting for 8 years in a district where race was considered no longer an issue. We accomplished good work over the years, exemplified in students' improved reading and writing performances and in raised teacher morale. Yet I was sure that the teachers' recurring request to know how to teach the low-achieving students could not be met without talking about race.

Clearly, I could have thought more carefully about how to broach this incendiary subject. I took for granted the years of good will between the teachers and me. They had come to trust that the workshops were for them—that together, as a group, we would determine what they needed to improve their practice, and I would provide the resources. In earlier years, privately I had asked black and white teacher leaders in the group about raising race as an issue, and they had warned me away from stirring up the tenuous social equilibrium we had achieved. I had been even more strongly told by the black associate superintendent to stick to curriculum and "not bring race into it." Before I arrived, the three high schools from which the teachers came had a long history of competitive and political divisiveness, some of it around issues of race, which the study group aimed to overcome—their way. They had not spoken to each other in the years before the study group, unless to complain, and they certainly did not collaborate. That had changed because they wanted it to for the sake of their students, and now I was talking about shaking things up again.

If I had given the subject more attention, I could have thought through what to say. More than choosing my words carefully, I could have predicted how each teacher might respond to this direction. If I doubted my ability to predict, then I might have cautiously opened a conversation about race and their teaching to discern how they thought and felt about it. Of my many missteps, two are most relevant here. One was my assumption that I already knew enough to broach the issue in the way

I did: announcing that it was time to take on race. The other error was in not allowing the teachers their rightful role. After all, we had remained together because they assumed, as they should, that they had an equal say in what we were doing. I did not have the right to make a unilateral announcement.

Although I felt intimidated and chastened, through reflection I learned a great deal from the tensions in the conversation that day. I was reminded of a number of tenets: how easy it is to assume, and how counterproductive those assumptions can be; that educators, like most people, feel threatened when asked to focus on unacknowledged tensions; and that the teaching of students most in need won't improve unless the difficult issues around difference are engaged. Retrospective reflection is key because I was too caught up in the moment to be able to monitor what I was saying and doing.

As do all professional educators, I brought to my analysis of this occurrence the knowledge I had acquired from similar cases over many years. Through hundreds of tense professional encounters, I had come to understand how uncomfortable and dangerous dialogues about racial and cultural difference can be. Even with years of experience, it remains difficult for school- and university-based teachers to build reliable ways of interacting to increase intercultural relationships and understanding. It shouldn't surprise us, then, that novice teachers feel uncomfortable talking about issues of difference, especially about students culturally unlike themselves who have difficulty with school, even when they believe in the necessity of those conversations to improve intercultural communication. This attraction-avoidance dilemma characterizes the awkward classroom moments involving cultural differences that arise as I'm teaching my pre-service teachers.

One moment that quickly comes to mind, case number two, was my effort, also a number of years ago, to promote conversations about encouraging reading of young adult fiction in which lesbian, gay, bisexual, or transgendered (LGBT) characters are protagonists. The vocal majority of my pre-service teachers resisted the idea as too controversial, claiming the communities in which they would teach would not accept these books and they could lose their jobs. (I had no way of knowing whether there were silent LGBT persons in the room.) They interpreted my request as a breach of the trust they had granted me as their guide to becoming successful teachers. I was thwarted in my attempts to engage them in dialogue. They saw no value in talking about a curriculum that would not be tolerated by their schools, their students, and their students' families. Because I had learned in earlier conversations of their commitment to socially just treatment, I pointed out that this way of positioning the problem conflicted with their professional values. They would be dismissing the interests and needs of the LGBT students they would undoubtedly have in class and be compromising a significant proportion of the population. They still would not consider my argument, saying instead that they would read a novel if they had to but thought it was a waste of time as there were so many other important things they should be learning. This stance, a step away from the LGBT issue, gave us the opening to talk about what as English teachers they should be prioritizing as important curriculum, what challenges complicate their acting on those priorities, and how they could and should resolve them. Although this topic skirted the LGBT issue, students were willing to speak about their individual beliefs and values regarding curriculum in general, which I considered a short distance from novels about cultural minorities. The conversation was at least moving in the direction I thought it should go. In some classes, that takes more time than others. And in some it doesn't happen.

A constructivist theory of teacher education posits that repeatedly engaging pre-service teachers in dialogues evoked from tense moments like this one positions them to build discursive tools and strategies for opening meaningful dialogues in their own classrooms. Through immersion, they can build confidence in and facility with conversing about risky topics. When they learn from such interactions, they become more inclined to view tense classroom moments as opportunities to engage students and promote learning. Pre-service teachers' willingness to acknowledge such encounters and reflect on them hinges on whether they can make productive use of their reflections as Monica, her colleagues, and I had done. Otherwise, those spaces are too uncomfortable and not worth their while to inhabit. In teacher education, many of us have been successful with telling, and even showing, teachers what they should be doing so that diversity can become an asset in their classrooms. We promote the principles of culturally relevant pedagogy and critical pedagogy, which direct teachers to awaken their students to their political positions in society. We provide curriculum and lesson plans that affirm students' own languages and cultural values. However, we seem to have been far less successful in providing teachers with the tools to understand *how* to enact those principles and curriculums in situated practices. Establishing pedagogical practices for teaching to and with diversity so that difference becomes an opportunity for all to learn remains a continuing challenge for us and for our students.

As we know, for teachers, understanding *how* means making good discursive choices to guide the dialogue. Such choices depend on recognizing momentary tensions in ways that afford acting to effectively engage them. This requires the ability to react on the fly, to talk ahead of one's conscious thinking. Such pedagogical skill is not easily built. It requires a disposition to focus on challenges one might otherwise avoid and to conceptualize those challenges in ways that make sense for each situation. It also requires continual attention to the quandaries of what to say or do next to keep the dialogue going.

When, in good faith, teachers can identify and explain the sources of discomfort with the goal of maintaining dialogue, they are much more likely to become adept at keeping them going. Monica and her colleagues voiced their concerns so as to keep our professional relationship authentically alive. My pre-service teachers became more adroit with my dialoguing mode of teaching and of their learning, and more predisposed to being strategic in their choices about what to say and do. They may not have been convinced by my way of thinking, but they learned how to respond to what I was saying so all of us could be heard and understood. They developed a language for dialoguing about difficult issues. They became attentive to keeping opportunities for conversing open with their own students. These were vital propensities for teaching that framed diversity as an asset.

## NARRATIVES, PEDAGOGY, AND PROFESSIONAL KNOWLEDGE

Those propensities were buoyed by the power of story. Monica and her colleagues and my pre-service teachers in these two cases relied on experiential narratives to explain and justify their positions. For pre- and in-service teachers, narrative is a way of becoming and being professional. They talk and think in story. They store their knowledge as narrative cases. They relate conditions and situations through storied descriptions of what did, can, or should take place. In the second case, my pre-service students' hypothetical narratives were powerful envisionings of being called on the carpet by a hostile administration. If I had provided a counternarrative, one that competed with the fear-laden pull of their story, I might have been more successful.

I missed an opportunity. Understanding my novice and experienced teachers' narratives as they spill out during classroom dialogues and providing immediate counternarratives are central to effective dialogic pedagogy. As a teacher educator, my job is to make use of storied ways of representing knowledge in our field, so as to help my students envision other, more productive possibilities. This constant challenge requires that, on the spot, I turn my situated practices in other contexts with other pre- and in-service teachers into stories that suit the current dialogue. More than that, in my stories, students should be able to recognize the knowledge and ideas applicable for the classroom situation in which they teach. This is a formidable task, one I usually feel I have insufficiently accomplished.

Case number three illustrates what I mean. It is another tense moment, again in my "Teaching of English" methods course, required for secondary English certification. This time, I provide a transcript of the moment in the conversation when things became awkward. Zerrick, a novice teacher, challenged my claim that a strategy for generating student interest in writing an essay would work with the students he was student teaching. Notice how the situation reflects a stance regarding issues of student participation, complicating cultural difference, and ethical or moral imperative.

Lesley:   Have your students take a stance about something that they feel strongly about. Before they read Romeo and Juliet, show them provocative parts of the DeCaprio movie and practice writing brief arguments.

Zerrick:  If I tell my students to do that, they wouldn't do it.

Lesley:   Why not?

Zerrick:  They don't care about writing essays. It's more boring school stuff. The students in that [video] class wanted to know how, but my students don't write essays. Grades aren't a big deal to them. They're used to failing English.

Zerrick and I have created a tense moment I frequently encounter—what I call "the standoff." Zerrick was reacting to the Annenberg video[2] I showed the class in an effort to illustrate what is pedagogically possible with urban student writers. A black high school teacher in the video is teaching writing to her impressively engaged black high school students. Zerrick, who is also black, has responded to my suggestion of an assignment that might provoke similar student participation with reasons for why it wouldn't work in his particular situation, with students who are inured to performing poorly in English classes. Cultural differences are complicated because Zerrick, a successful middle-class black college graduate, is teaching mostly working-class black students, and I am white and from a working-class background.

What we said next is a common beginning to discussions in my classroom. I ask for evidence of claims, and students respond with narratives, many of them experiential.

Lesley:   How do you know that?

Zerrick:  At the beginning of the unit, I taught paragraph writing so I could start out small before asking them to write essays. I had really good lessons planned, where I took them step by step through every part of writing a paragraph. And I made it fun, too, by bringing in pizza and having them write a review of it. They loved the pizza. The writing not so much. They wrote like second graders.

Zerrick's first story is a telling of what had happened when he taught his lesson that focuses on his lesson and their performance. But he followed this brief narrative with more stories about particular students of his and their circumstances that were at once unique and yet meant to represent the typical reasons his students could not write like high school students and why they no longer wanted to try. These narratives were sympathetic to the students, critical of the circumstances visited on them, and demanding of me and the institution of teacher education I represent. Through his stories, he took a decidedly moral stance, and he wanted me to help him do something, something ethical, to rectify the situation.

I wish that I had been able to meet that challenge in the moment, but I couldn't offer appropriate complementary narratives of my own to illustrate how to fruitfully engage students in the lesson, understand the complicating cultural issues, and take ethical actions. This is not uncommon, sometimes because I haven't taught in that particular context or because I cannot draw on the right story for that moment. In fact, I rarely use stories from my own teaching practice and only as dramatic punctuation. The narratives I usually tell are borrowed from English education and literacy curriculum sources—from textbooks and professional resources, expert accounts, research studies, and the Internet or videos. For example, I describe how someone else performed as described in a well-respected book on the subject, such as what secondary reading specialist Kylene Beers (2002) describes as a successful reading encounter. I take this tack because I have learned that, although teachers enjoy stories from my own experience as a teacher, which carry a great deal of social and some instructional weight, they are more convinced by the knowledge in these other sources. Now that I am no longer a practicing high school English teacher, I have lost a great deal of my "street" credibility.

I pride myself on the wealth of storied materials I can draw from, yet once again I am chastened by their inadequacy. Although the narratives of classroom life that appear in these sources are more influential, they are limited in their usefulness. Stories of particular places, people, and circumstances are a poor match for the unique circumstances in most classrooms. Teachers know that, and they distrust the implicit assumption in teacher education that such examples can sufficiently suit other situations. This problem of transferability is critical. Teachers tell me that during an actual classroom teaching situation, they never recall specific case knowledge or prescriptive strategies from their teacher education classes, not even in their first years of teaching. The gap between what happened in other classrooms and is now happening in theirs appears too wide and is complicated by numerous official and unofficial policies (Spillane,

2004).[3] This mis- or indirect-match condition is a major source of their undervaluing of teacher education as sufficient preparation for teaching.

Such testimonies have given me pause. How can my discussions with them shrink this gap by helping teachers relate what's happening in the instructional example classroom with what happens in their own (J. Foster, 2004). I have to keep in mind that as "street-level professionals" (Lipsky, 1980), teachers shoulder huge responsibilities and serve many masters. So, managing tense, personally fraught topics having to do with cultural difference and ethical stance adds to an already heavy pedagogical load for them and for me. I have discovered that the weight of this load becomes more manageable when the language of our teaching and learning becomes more transparent. Hence, the value in understanding narratives as central to pedagogical success and the purpose for this volume. Each chapter aims to say something of use about the role that narrative plays in teaching with diversity.[4]

## WHAT DO WE MEAN BY NARRATIVE?

Although each chapter presents its own take on narrative, I provide a brief introductory overview because "narrative," like "context," is a word that is used as though everyone knows what is meant by it and means the same thing. These words are part of teachers' and teacher educators' commonly used lexicon; they take for granted that a narrative is a story, a retelling of something that happened. The ubiquity of this common-sense view of story and its taken-for-granted status are good reasons for a much closer look. Of course, a narrative is a story. However, ways of understanding the importance of narrative in the construction of knowing (White, 1981), of self (Bakhtin, 1981), and of knowledge (Bruner, 1986) make it possible for us to think of narrative in ways that can generate more productive teaching practices. If, for example, I had talked with Zerrick about the narratives he was telling, what would I have said that would have enhanced that teaching moment? What would I have said narratives were, and how would I have described what his were doing? What would be the reason for pointing those elements out? What could I have accomplished?

I could have explained to Zerrick that scholars who study oral narratives notice that narrators make general points about themselves and about the world through the stories they tell. The oral narrative is a way the narrator circumscribes and structures life activities or what happens/happened. They allow speakers to illustrate their point of view or more general claims about the world. A whole narrative or story often articulates a single moral stance or overall theme regarding what is right and wrong, what good and proper people should do, and/or how persons should comport themselves in the world. I could have asked Zerrick to consider the particular, consequential view of people and events inscribed in his narratives. What might this dialogue with him have accomplished? As I have written elsewhere, it is important for teachers to understand the power of their narratives to engage, discourage, identify, and shape students and their participation (Rex, Murnen, Hobbs, & McEachen, 2002). My hope would be that Zerrick might have eventually come to understand how his narratives about his students and their narratives about themselves are central to classroom teaching and learning (Hicks, 1991) and consequential.

Theories about narrative as a way to construct knowing, the known, and the knower can depict narrative discourse between teachers and students as the bridge among student learning, cognition, and identity (Bruner, 1986; Geertz, 1973). Other theories about the classroom as a learning culture view classroom storytellers and their audience as constructing normative ways of acting, believing, perceiving, and evaluating each other and their knowledge (Rex, 2006b). In classroom social cultures, stories are powerful symbolic conversational texts with consequences for learning and the learner. They construct and embody classroom membership or exclusion; they represent and construct understanding, confusion, agreement, or dispute among tellers and hearers. As members of a social culture, through self-reflexive classroom narratives, teachers and students attempt to understand what they know and need to know, how they are being viewed, and who they need to be in their current situation.

This narrative-based, culture-constitutive, self-reflexive process is also a useful way to represent the activity of classroom teaching and learning for pre-service teachers. They can understand that when teachers tell stories, even when the stories are not explicitly or intentionally instructional, they tell them in a way that represents a view of what counts as appropriate social and academic knowledge and performance. Teachers can observe, discuss, and experiment with how narratives in their classroom talk compel as well as construct and impede student learning. They can comprehend that as part of larger, continuing classroom dialogues, members' stories purposefully build on prior narratives and influence what talk may come next. They can assess the value-laden, right-wrong depictions that tellers make of themselves, others, and "realities." That is, they can examine what their narratives communicate about how teachers and students should act and what behavior, information, and points of view they should value, believe in, and know about.

This volume has been written to assist teacher educators in making the shift from seeing narratives as transparent storytelling to deploying narratives as powerful pedagogy. It takes a particular view of narrative that grows out of a sociolinguistic approach informed by Labov (1972; Labov & Waletsky, 1967), who defined *narrative* as a series of at least two temporally sequenced and causally linked clauses (see Juzwik, 2006). Labov further suggested that oral narratives allow speakers to illustrate their point of view, or more general claims about the world, through a narrative feature he called *evaluation*. From a sociolinguistic perspective, evaluation is a linguistic category including those linguistic means by which points of view are signified by narrators. Labov and subsequent sociolinguistic researchers (Linde, 1993; Polanyi, 1985; Wortham, 2001) elaborated a range of linguistic and paralinguistic resources that narrators use to make more general points about themselves and about the world, from metalinguistic markers (e.g., *said* vs. *protested*) to phonological emphasis (e.g., louder volume) and parallelism (e.g., repetition at various levels of text and context). *Moral stance*, or *moral stance taking*, in oral narrative genres (as discussed by Ochs & Capps, 2001) is a more global application of the term *evaluation*. Where a narrative typically includes multiple indicators of evaluation (e.g., expressive intonation, repetition, comparators), a narrative taken as a whole often articulates a single moral stance or overall theme regarding what is right and wrong, what good and proper people should do, and/or how persons should comport themselves in the world. (cf. Juzwik, Nystrand, Kelly, & Sherry, 2008, pp. 1116-1117)

By understanding narratives through these lenses as ubiquitous teaching practices laden with instructional messages, instructive in and of themselves, pre-service teachers can see why analyzing narratives is part of their teacher education curriculum. They can understand that they and their students have sensible (often unconscious) reasons for telling the stories they do. They can know that, on the basis of classroom narratives, students choose whether, when, and how to participate and evaluate the success of their participation. Perhaps most important they can understand that, over time, the frequency, duration, and kinds of narratives that they and their students tell and the occasions on which they tell them shape how students think they need to present themselves, what students count as knowledge, and how students display achievement in their classroom.

## NARRATIVE RESEARCH IN EDUCATION

A reasonable question is whether teaching new and experienced teachers to better understand how narratives function is worth the effort, especially given the demands on teachers' and teacher educators' time to achieve other objectives. It seems like an arcane skill, more academic than practical. Yet I have become convinced that such knowledge is at the heart of understanding how to productively engage the cultural diversity of students in teaching and learning practices so that all students are provided with equitable access to learning. I have been convinced by my own research and that of co-editor Mary Juzwik, which draws from a deep reservoir of narrative studies in education and sociolinguistics.

For many years, I have attempted to explore and understand questions of participation, difference, and moral stance in ways that would contribute to practice. That has meant continually combining theories and methods to create new perspectives and methodologies for informing classroom teaching and learning. Sometimes it has meant reconceptualizing the problem or issue. That led me to consider pedagogical narratives as a way to view the problem of inequitable access to instruction (Rex et al., 2002). In reviewing the literature at the time, I learned how little research had been done in this area. Yet in researching teachers' pedagogical narratives, I was impressed by how influential they were. Teachers' stories inscribed worlds, beliefs, and identities that consequentially positioned their students' participation and performance. In my study, the teachers' stories, mostly object lessons, presented contrasting visions of education and accomplishment. Each teacher's narratives appealed to a particular demographic of students, such that one teacher's stories would not have appealed to students in the other teacher's class. Because both teachers were involved in the research, their new awareness led them to seriously reflect on their narrative practices. They subsequently reinforced some of their narratives and their applications and changed others. This experience and other research explorations prepared me to recognize the value in the research that grounds this book.

In a series of narrative studies in secondary English classrooms, Mary has drawn attention to the multiple functions of oral narratives in classroom interaction. One line of her work illustrates how teacher narratives shaped instruction thematically centered on the Holocaust and was a powerful, at times even dangerous, force shaping classroom interaction and ultimately what students come to learn about the Holocaust (Juzwik, 2004a, 2004b, 2006, 2009). In another study in a culturally and linguistically diverse English classroom, she linked narrative talk to discussion, showing how narratives could be used to prime, sustain, ratify, and amplify discussions about literature (Juzwik et al., 2008) by incorporating students' previous life experiences. Other recent work on classroom narratives focuses on the functions of classroom narrative in diverse elementary classrooms, including child (Martinez-Roldan, 2003; Poveda, 2002) and teacher (Poveda, 2003) storytelling practices.

The work in narrative draws from scholarship and research in linguistics and discourse analysis. Since the 1960s, social science researchers have attempted to represent facets of classrooms' social spheres for the purpose of improving education.[5] Discourse studies have been seminal in understanding classroom teaching and learning interactions. Research utilizing discourse, or language in use, has described the social and power dimensions of classroom teaching. These representations portray each classroom as a unique, dynamically shifting social landscape and educational culture. To this point, teacher education has been only peripherally influenced by this research. The field has just recently begun to benefit from more direct and focused applications of these theories and methodologies.[6]

## CONSIDERING PARTICIPATION, DIFFERENCE, AND ETHICS

Mary and I are making a shift toward a more direct and pragmatic focus with this volume. As discourse analysis and classroom narrative analysis have been demonstrated to be well suited to understanding issues of participation, difference, and ethical responsibility—key to improving pedagogy—we use these three facets, in the form of questions, to anchor the remaining chapters:

*How can teachers engage and sustain diverse students' **participation** in productive knowledge-building?*

*How can **differences** in classrooms become opportunities for all to learn?*

*How are **ethical responsibility and moral stance** implicated in efforts to improve student participation and respect difference?*

Unless teacher education practices address these three questions, the gap between what we tell our teachers to do and help them understand how to do so will remain wide.

### How Can Teachers Engage and Sustain Diverse Students' Participation in Productive Knowledge-Building?

In my inquiries toward improving classroom teaching and learning, I continually return to "participation" as a central issue (e.g., Rex, 2000, 2001, 2002, 2003, 2006a, 2006b; Rex & McEachen, 1999; Rex, Murnen, Hobbs, & McEachen, 2002). Participation has come to mean the challenge of initiating and sustaining students' individual and social engagement in classroom subject matter learning activity. This is a multifaceted and complicated challenge. In much of my research, I have chosen to explore those facets from the teacher's perspective. The teacher exerts institutional authority for the classroom and authorizes some of the different ways students act as learners. In these authoritative roles, as the social mediator of difference, the teacher determines who engages and participates. Students engage and interact with the teacher and other students when they recognize the ways of being, acting, and knowing the teacher authorizes as meaningful. Consequently, participation is particularly a problem of meaning—students recognizing the work of the class as meaningful, constructing meaning for themselves if and when they engage in it, and sustaining meaning construction from day to day. It is also a problem of identity—of students recognizing themselves as the kinds of people they think they are and want to be, and of being recognized by other class members in those ways. It is a problem of social relationships—of students acting as social beings to enact and reinforce latent social networks and construct new ones. Attached to all of these facets of the participation challenge is the issue of value—of students recognizing the activities, meaning, social roles and relationships, and identities they are performing as imbued with beliefs, dispositions, and values that are their own.

For teachers to understand how to sustain meaningful participation requires them to assume responsibility for being the mediators for what occurs in the classroom. For teachers to sustain equitable meaningful participation requires them to understand how to mediate the productive participation of ALL their students. The authors' shared assumption is that, by understanding how narratives work as interactive dialogic events, teachers can better understand the issues of identity, social relationship, and knowledge construction. The chapters focus most particularly on identity or self and social relationship within the pursuit of knowledge building. Further, they recommend a particular epistemology for observing narrative interactions—that is, that narratives should be observed as dialogic sociocultural work and that the methods of sociolinguistic analysis can facilitate this sociocultural approach to narrative. They assume that if researchers and teacher educators take on this sociocultural lens and develop sociolinguistic methodologies, they will better understand how to promote cross-cultural communicative practices. At the center of all the chapters is a concern for the moral stances that narrators take with their stories and a belief that moral stances are where we should be fixing our attention. They view these as productive sites for educating teachers about their own and their students' positive and negative "othering."

## How Can Differences in Classrooms Become Opportunities for all to Learn?

In this volume, "othering" is meant as an act taken when one notices difference in other people's action and attributes an unjust or offensive identity to it. Originating in the writings of G. W. F. Hegel (1969, 1979), the concept has evolved in existential philosophy, postcolonialism, and psychoanalysis. In education, Gloria Ladson-Billings (1995) and others (e.g., DeCuir & Dixson, 2004) have used the construct to great effect. For our purposes, people who "other," whether intentionally or not, are judged to be securing their own positive identity at the expense of stigmatizing another. In this volume, we address othering in teacher education as an act of identity recognition and social relationship-building during teaching and learning activity. Acts of othering are related to differences in the values, beliefs, and dispositions of those involved in a particular situation.

This is a book about one approach to seeing difference and doing something besides "othering." Our premise is that we have to recognize and act on differences in human identity in a way that makes possible working with them positively and productively. All manner of human difference is othered, from body configuration to income to ethnicity, to whether one buys clothes at Neiman Marcus, T. J. Maxx, or a thrift store, to whether one speaks a variety of nonstandard English. As has been written about extensively, these social differences, located in familial and cultural patterns, are consequential for students, whether they are preservice teachers or their soon-to-be students.

We posit that for teachers to manage the tendency toward "othering" when presented with difference requires a professional stance toward interacting with students that is opportunistically open. Such openness allows what Kerschbaum refers to in her chapter, citing Bakhtin (1990, 1993), as "answerable engagement." An opportunistically open professional stance is important to create because not all differences are readily recognizable, and even those differences that at first sight may seem apparent may not be those that are most relevant in a particular interaction. Maintaining an open professional stance while learning how to make use of the knowledge generated through narrative and narrative analysis necessitates understanding differences as myriad, dynamic, and negotiated. This stance requires us to hold ourselves responsible for learning about, and with, others because learning about others is not a passive, receptive activity but a highly interactive one. Looking for opportunities to engage students in ways meaningful to them requires vigilance and agency.

To approach diversity with an open opportunistic professional stance requires the disposition that difference is a fundamental, inevitable, and potentially productive or divisive aspect of the human social condition. Differences exist between us and our closest friends and family members, as well as between us and our students and their students. Difference is not a static circumstance. We know that what seems similar and different shifts with changes in setting, situation, timing, and who is present. Negotiating difference is what each of us does when we refer to our actions as communicating, advising, or teaching. Making an opportunity out of difference is what teachers do when they teach effectively.

Another principle of this book is the view that interacting with students in ways that they perceive as meaningful is a constant challenge that has been the undoing of many curriculums intended to promote equitable learning. Acting in ways that all members of an interaction perceive as meaningful requires keen perception and vigilance as well as a disposition to continually learn about the dispositions, stances, experiences, and values of others. We assume that we can never come to wholly understand the positions and lives of others—to fully walk in their shoes or to know their culture. To think that educators can is counterproductive to our aim with this book. Likewise, the view of humanity as universal, that at some levels all human beings are the same, ignores the influential role of culture and enculturation in classroom teaching and learning. Scholars of whiteness and critical race theories have pointed out the need to give up these traditional dominant "white" ways of thinking. After all, understanding that at the DNA level all people are the same has not eliminated classist, ethnocentric, or racist ways of thinking and behaving.

A more promising principle to inform an open opportunistic professional stance, we think, is the reverse stance—to assume that we can never fully know anyone else's situation, history, or experience. Accepting this premise of incomplete knowledge allows the viewer to assume a stance that is open to opportunity. It creates an interactive space for learning and for the possibility of acting in a way that is recognized as meaningful. Keeping teaching and learning interactions open to opportunities for meaningful engagement also implies respect for differences and for the right of others to their differences. By focusing on narrative interaction in this volume, we carry forward these premises to mean that teachers and students have a right to voice their viewpoints through their narratives. However, because narratives are so consequential in classroom teaching, it is a responsibility of teacher educators to help teachers reflect on their narratives—especially on those that make them feel most uncomfortable—and on how they react to their students' narratives.

## How Are Ethical Responsibility and Moral Stance Implicated in Efforts to Improve Participation and Respect Difference?

Narratives that teachers and students tell in their classrooms reflect their own views regarding what is moral, good and bad, right and wrong. They also, as Betsy Rymes and Stanton Wortham explain (Chapter 3, this volume), tell listeners how to behave and where they are positioned in an implicit moral hierarchy. In the stories that teachers tell, characters and their actions may be rendered as appropriate, dutiful, outrageous, complicit, or untenable. Such teacher depictions carry a force that can by degrees challenge, disdain, reinforce, or applaud those held by students. This can, in turn, influence whether students choose to participate and how they self-identify if they do. Likewise, students' personal narratives provide fragile platforms for social and instructional negotiation of difference. This moral weight, and its impact when building a classroom culture of respect for difference and positive meaningful engagement, makes classroom narratives impossible to ignore. Narratives make the private public. By integrating personal values into social instructional work, ethical problems are inevitable, and we concur with Lee Schulman (2002) that educators have an obligation to examine the impact of this effect on students.[7] We claim this obligation as an ethical one; it would be unethical not to assist teachers in the observation of the impact of their own practice.

## Distinguishing Between Moral Stances and Professional Ethics

In addition to illustrating what we mean by the opportunities and challenges of an open professional stance, this volume highlights the moral ambiguities and ethical problems generated by classroom-based narratives. In this section, I provide an extended exploration of issues related to the third question because dealing with moral and ethical dilemmas is the most fraught aspect of using narrative analysis in teacher education—and, therefore, the most difficult and the most important. To provide some clarity, I begin by making a working distinction between "professional" ethics or ethical responsibility and individual morality or moral behavior.[8] These distinctions, although overdrawn, should assist in making sense of the chapters in this volume.

In my practice as a teacher educator, I have found an overstated distinction between morals and ethics a useful common language for putting the issue out for discussion. As soon as the teachers and I apply the distinction to analyze classroom teaching situations, they see why ethics and morality cannot be reduced to binaries, which in turn opens a conversation about why taking moral stands is so fraught for teachers.

For example, teachers who had to decide whether to report a minor's pregnancy to her parents or a teacher colleague's intimate relations with an adult student have experienced the difficulties of separating out personal moral values from professional ethical codes. Distinctions between the constructs are also troubled throughout pertinent scholarship, so I do not draw on experience, scholarship, or research to distinguish them for our purposes in this volume. Instead I offer a working definition to distinguish between personal morals and professional ethics. I have evolved the definition to address the predicament I encountered in my own teaching when my pre-service teachers asked, "How am I to respect what is meaningful to my students when it conflicts with what I think is right?" or "When a student says something that is so disrespectful or insulting to me or another student, how am I supposed to react without shutting them down?" I have found that distinguishing between personal and professional roles is useful. Assuming the role of teacher as a member of a profession requires each individual to develop an awareness of what an individual considers her own sense of what is right in a given situation and what as a teacher is the right course of action. Of course, that distinction is not easy or simple to make, and the work of making it never ends for the practicing reflective teacher. But that is the point.

Morals and ethics, for my teacher educator purposes, can be described as differing in several respects, although both stances hold that individuals can and should arrive at right and proper decisions to act in the face of consequential difference. Morality implies values invoked by individuals that usually relate to a deity, religion, or philosophy. Moral belief systems hold to ideals of goodness and principles for measuring behavior in relation to those ideals. Ethics as they relate to a profession such as teaching are shared understandings by members of a social group organized by virtue of being members of the same profession. Although morals serve to guide an individual's personal beliefs and behaviors, ethics provide a commonly agreed to set of principles by which professionals can assess how to act. This ethical set of beliefs by which all members of the profession are dutifully connected, usually called a Code of Conduct or Code of Ethics, provides a set of guidelines as to how they and their fellow professionals can reasonably be expected to act in the same or similar conditions.

For example, we speculate that a principle in our pedagogical Ethical Code of Conduct might be, as it is in medicine, to do no harm. The next step would be to establish criteria to guide teachers in assessing whether harm is likely in a given situation under particular conditions. The set of rules and guidelines would strive to be personal morals-neutral, in the sense that they would not draw directly from a person's religious or philosophical stance. However, each teacher's pedagogy will be guided by her personal beliefs and values as well as by a professional code of ethics. While teaching "Romeo and Juliet," for example, she may discuss the lovers' suicide pact with her students. Undoubtedly, she will hold a personal moral stance about the right to take one's own life. She may consider it a terrible sin, a human right, or an unwise choice. Or she could be ambivalent. Regardless of her personal moral stance, her conduct in leading the discussion and the consequences for her students should be consistent with a teaching code of ethics.

Because no single, uniform code of ethics exists for teachers, I propose a pragmatic test. Would a random selection of teachers, perhaps those in any teacher education course, who observed the suicide discussion consider the teacher's practices ethical—that is, not a danger to her students? If I were one of those observers, would I be concerned if a teacher *solely* waxed lyrical about the romance of the act, made dismissive light of suicide as a romantic literary technique, or declared Romeo and Juliet forever barred from righteous forgiveness? Couldn't a single stance impelled by moral conviction, whether conscious or not, be potentially damaging to students? A teacher rarely knows whether her students have brushed up against suicide and what that has led them to believe. Statistics tell us that suicide is already the second leading cause of death among teenagers.

A pragmatic working professional Code of Ethics for teaching, therefore, can be part of teachers' self-regulatory sounding board, one that allows a variety of personal beliefs. Actions can appear ethical as well as moral (if they share religious principles), amoral (if not religiously addressed), and immoral (if denounced by a particular religious orientation). Similarly, moral actions can be ethical, nonethical, or unethical. The professional ethics test can help teachers regulate their teaching of diverse—multi-abled, multiracial, multi-ethnic, and multicultural—students in learning with and from each other. This morality-ethics framework brings into view for teachers the tensions that may arise between their own moral values and their professional code. The distinctions also frame a way of talking about the inevitable tensions that arise between their students' values and their own or their profession's.

To create a similar opportunity to address ways of framing issues of moral stance, chapter authors also complicate the distinction. Kerschbaum (Chapter 5, this volume), for example, theorizes an "ethical responsibility" of students and teachers for each other, what she calls "answerable engagement," which incorporates what Juzwik (2004c) has called the morally weighty moment of being in everyday interaction. Based on Bakhtin's (1990, 1993) ethical theories, answerability places responsibility on individuals to respond to others and to hold themselves accountable for those utterances. Kerschbaum's and Juzwik's views of the moment as morally weighty is what we teacher educators want our teachers to understand and believe. We want them to exercise that responsibility with the understanding that value-laden individual belief systems are in continual negotiation with the moral awareness demanded of the social citizen.

## THE ORGANIZATION OF THE CHAPTERS

### Beginning and Ending With Teachers

A book for teacher educators about using narrative study to explore opportunistic tensions in diverse classrooms should, we think, begin and end with the perspectives of school-based teachers, especially those in circumstances in which race is a key factor. In this volume, high school English teachers Steve Bodnar and Andrea Zellner speak for those teachers.[9] Their opening and closing commentaries frame the chapters written by the teacher educators and researchers. Bodnar's and Zellner's comments on these chapters ground the other authors' key ideas and anchor the volume in the teachers' everyday subjective spaces. Their commentaries remind the reader that school-based teachers are situated differently in their uses of narrative from the ways we are demonstrating in this volume. Keeping these differences in mind is helpful in understanding that teacher educators, who find our ideas useful, will be asking teachers, who are adept narrators, to apply theories of language to reconceptualize the ways they think of and use narratives.

As you will see, Bodnar and Zellner are already narrative thinkers, reflectors, and writers. Their commentaries reflect two different framings of narrative thinking about practice, which we have located to raise particular questions about narratives for readers. Bodnar's, the first, reflects a teacher who thinks about narrative as literary form and style; who is concerned with characters, conflicts, scenes, settings, and themes; and who relies on the semiosis of narratives in his classroom. Bodnar posits the worth of viewing teaching as a web of narratives and of learning how to use narratives to transform.

His way of framing narrative evokes rich tensions for the reader to consider. In a narrative report from the field, he illuminates what he considers the common everyday grief and successes that arise from stories that teachers tell themselves about their students. At the end of Bodnar's narrative, we prompt readers to consider five issues we think are important to what we do as teacher educators: transformation, "real" talk, discipline-based narratives, ethics, and moral stance. These are the first of many end-of-chapter questions throughout the volume.

Andrea Zellner closes the volume by emphasizing the humanity of narrative and its various consequential functions in her classroom. In English curricula, literary narratives carry aesthetic and cultural weight as well as human meaning. The novels and stories students are expected to read may or may not make their participation easy, difficult, or impossible. The students' challenge is to establish a meaningful link between their personal narratives and literary narratives. The English teacher's responsibility is to help students bridge distances in meaning between the two. Dialogic classroom narratives become the sites of these negotiated meanings.

Zellner well describes the consequences for teachers and students of these negotiations of personal meaning and cultural and literary literacy: tensions erupt. She provides readers with her own questions for their reflection. For example: Should teachers correct the language in which personal stories are told? At what point should they be relayed in the "language of commerce"? Should literary narratives more likely to evoke personal narratives be those that are read? Coming at the end of the volume, Zellner's commentary revoices the reality of the teacher's responsibility as cultural mediator, her role in creating and managing powerful and irresolvable tensions, and the ethical dilemmas she juggles as cultural translator.

Bodnar's and Zellner's commentaries illuminate the investment in ways of thinking about narrative English teachers bring to narrative analysis. For English teachers, love for literature is frequently a main reason for wanting to be educators. It is the discipline of choice. Yet the commentaries convey that narrative is more than subject matter. For Bodner and Zellner, story exemplifies their way of being professional educators. It is the way they think and talk about who they are as teachers. The move from how teachers think about story to how we propose teacher educators ask them to think about it will require careful and sustained attention. We ask English teachers to deemphasize literary conceptualizations of story and personal investment in story as a mode of identity and put a linguistic orientation—how language in use performs—front and center. That means we ask them to step back and critically analyze their own narratives—their representations of their professional work, competence, and identity. In reorienting teachers' approaches to narratives, the stakes are high.

## Bringing Theory to Situated Practice

Chapter 3 by linguists Betsy Rymes and Stanton Wortham begins this reorientation. It pivots the reader from a teacher's to a teacher educator's perspective on narratives. As preparation for the Johnson, Kerschbaum, and Juzwik chapters, Rymes and Wortham explain the constructs available to teacher educators who utilize narrative analysis. They offer key concepts for using narrative analysis to explore issues of participation, difference, and moral and ethical dilemmas, and they outline methods for empirically studying the critical elements in play in any narrating event. They focus on the analytical roles of truth, power, morality, and individual agency that the chapter authors use. These four constructs thread through (out) the rest of the volume as analytical lenses for observing classroom narratives. By focusing on what analysts understand as truth, power, morality, and an individual's freedom to act, Rymes and Wortham's chapter provides language for talking and thinking about participation, difference, and ethics as a narrated phenomenon.

## The Moral Stances That Teachers Create in Their Autobiographical Narratives

Literacy educator Amy Johnson (Chapter 4, this volume) introduces teacher educators to a collection of methods they can utilize to reflect on their own and their students' autobiographical narratives, and on their interactions with their students while they tell them. Johnson illustrates how they can provide informative layered interpretations that promote critical reflection. She points out the delicacy of bringing the pre-service teacher's experience into dialogue with broader social issues and the difficulty of doing so without dishonoring the pre-service teacher or her history.

Johnson's chapter describes how, in narrative conversations between teachers and teacher educators, moral stances can be rendered malleable through exploration of their ethical consequences. By heightening pre-service teachers' awareness of their moral stances in relation to larger social equity issues, tensions and conflicts arise that teacher educators can use for instruction while critically assessing their own "communicative palettes." Acknowledging this as a necessary and inevitable responsibility, Johnson argues, "telling stories with teacher educators may enable teachers to develop and enact certain identities; and reframe their stories, and thus, reframe their viewpoints." She claims that this is the exact work of teacher educators: to prompt their students to "zoom out from their immediate experiences, situate these experiences within broader social contexts, and shift the onus from the individual to the institution." This is the professional turn, to understand and be disposed toward the ethical responsibilities of the teaching profession. Johnson illustrates through her analysis of a pre-service teacher's narrative how teacher educators can use narrative analysis to move their students toward that goal. The first strategic step is understanding that one's pedagogical discourse and curriculum choices communicate moral stances, and the second is to inhabit those stances in ways that are professionally ethical.

## Student Identity Marking and Social Positioning

Compositionist Stephanie Kerschbaum (Chapter 5, this volume) focuses on the narratives that students tell each other during a writing response group conversation. Kerschbaum observed the identity work of two university freshman writing students to see how they articulated and acknowledged their awareness of difference with each other. Kerschbaum's analyses demonstrate the richness of narrative analysis to illustrate marked differences in how narratives construct the "truth" of experience and the values and identities associated with them. Marked differences highlight how each young woman positioned herself and the other while the two interactively narrated their high school writing experiences. We are shown the young women performing braggadocio as socially acceptable complaint. We see in these co-joined narratives social relationship-building underway as each student commiserates with the other.

Through this comparative analysis, Kerschbaum's transcripts reveal the sophisticated yet delicate social dance that occurs among members of writing response groups. Each woman's narrative is generated from the need to maintain her own status without threatening the face of the other. Through Kerschbaum's marking, we can view the young women's narrative interaction as a demonstration of opportunistic open stances in social negotiation. Each young woman appears to have responded to difference in the other in a way that positions the other to be acknowledged for her stance while also providing space to present the self she wants to be in the interaction while keeping the classwork moving forward. The chapter presents their narratives as a dance of intertwined identification and differentiation in pursuit of successful academic performance. Kerschbaum's transcripts could be of use in a teacher education classroom to show how adeptly students with common goals but distinctively different cultural orientations and identities can productively socially negotiate. Nevertheless, as Kerschbaum points out, this dance has its limitations for using difference as opportune for learning in the classroom. Their conversation does not propel further discussion about their differences that could build a more informed collaboration to improve their writing. More important, Kerschbaum raises for consideration the limitations of spoken narratives as the sole or main source for pedagogical decisions.

## Dialogic Narratives for Understanding Culture

Drawing from her research-informed pedagogical experiment with narratives in her teacher education classroom, Mary Juzwik (Chapter 6, this volume) describes and unpacks morally weighty narratives about the Holocaust as an exercise in teaching about culture, which Juzwik hypothesizes is key to teaching to difference. Juzwik describes how she led her teachers in comparing the classroom narratives a student and teacher told during the course of a middle-school unit about the Holocaust. Whereas Johnson's chapter focused teachers on the moral weightiness of the narratives they tell, and what the stories tell about them, Juzwik's account illustrates the potential use of morally weighty dialogic class-room narratives between teachers and students in a teacher education setting. This account unpacks how to produce the critical discussions nec-essary for teachers to openly engage difference. Juzwik demonstrates the power of such dialogic narratives to reveal how individuals not only locate themselves culturally in narratives, but also how they draw on cul-tural resources and negotiate many cultural worlds. The analyses become a way to describe the classroom in which the stories are told as its own culture, building its own cultural processes for engaging morally weighty topics. The effect for the teachers is to "de-exoticize" the concept of cul-ture so they recognize culture in language and in the everyday. Another outcome is the possibility of developing a culturally situated view of the world and of the students in a teachers' classroom. By examining moral stance, Juzwik's teachers could consider different moral and evaluative stances in relation to cultural differences within classroom narratives.

## FINAL NOTE

Living within unavoidable problems of practice is one definition of the role of the teacher. Teachers learn to live within the tensions. Good teach-ers accept them as part of the professional role. Outstanding teachers make them fodder for learning. As teacher educators, our responsibility is to direct teachers to build the wherewithal to be outstanding and hold them to it. That means they become predisposed to take on the tensions and to have acquired the intellectual decision-making structures to make productive use of narratives.

While encouraging readers to be earnest in pursuing that goal, the chapters in this volume also reveal the complications that should give us pause. Not the least of these is what Jacquelien Bulterman-Bos (2008) has argued: that problems of practice visible in classroom narratives do not appear the same to those living within these tensions every day as they do to researchers, linguists, and teacher educators. Even when similarly named, descriptions of problems of practice vary depending on who does the describing, with whom, in what situation, and for what purpose. These variations can be purposefully and, I think, usefully categorized for teacher education in terms of differences in perspective, stance, accountability, and authority. Who is framing how we view the phenom-ena? What is their claim about it? How can that frame and claim be assessed? Who determines what counts?

Our intention has been to generate and mitigate tensions around the red flag topics of participation, difference, and ethics. We have done so by viewing these hot button issues through the lenses of truth, power, morality, and individual agency. This is a delicate and perhaps impossible balance. Any possible success hinges on the reader's willingness to accept a key assumption: that readers, as well as teachers, can and should take an open, opportunistic professional stance. I am continually reminded of how much vigilant attention that stance requires.

As I write this introduction and reflect on my practices as a teacher educator and researcher, I encounter continual ethical dilemmas. Am I denigrating or condescending in how I represent participants in my research? Am I positioning myself as the moral agent in relation to teacher education, to the narratives of my participants, and to the contents of their narratives? When I teach, does my language convey a moral superiority or a genuine interest in understanding ethical complications?

In this book, my co-editor, Mary Juzwik, and I have worked to avoid claiming an ethical high ground; we also have considered who has the potential to get harmed through the representations and interpretations we have appropriated for our purposes. Although we have tempered our textual discourse, we realize that no degree of rhetorical management will eliminate the probability that we have fallen short. Readers will read this text from their own stances and encounter tensions well beyond those we sought to produce. Our hope is that you will find those unintended tensions worth the effort.

## NOTES

1. Throughout this volume, I refer to races as black and white following the practices of teachers in the study group.
2. http://www.learner.org
3. Such strategic decisions are considered central to the work of teaching (Borko, Cone, Russo, & Shavelson, 1979; Feiman-Nemser & Floden, 1986) and exceedingly demanding due to the multiplicity, ambiguity, and variety of factors involved (Cochran-Smith & Lytle, 2006). It is commonly accepted in our field that teachers actively and uniquely interpret, construct, and reconstruct curriculum in every lesson they teach each day (Bredekamp, 1997; Connelly & Clandinin, 1988; Elbaz, 1981; Marsh, 2002; Shavelson & Stern, 1981).
4. Although the data and references to classroom life concern literacy teaching and learning, narrative analyses and representations reflect nondisciplinary-specific tensions. They provide conceptual and procedural resources to predispose pre- and in-service teachers to identify and reflect on tensions around differences that arise in all classrooms; to look at teacher and student narratives as sites for analyzing these tensions; and to make analyses that are satisfyingly useful in their practice.
5. Linguists, and others influenced by the turn toward language as key to understanding human phenomena, have played a dominant role in this trend. Researchers grounded in linguistic- and ethnographic-based traditions have explored language interactions as social phenomena in education. Drawing

from theories in linguistics, anthropology, sociology, philosophy, and education, researchers have conceived discourse, or language in use, as constituting and constitutive of school-based social contexts, social and academic identities, academic knowledge, and disciplinary practices, as well as classroom teaching and learning. This framework has provided new ways to examine the complex cognitive processes involved in student and teacher oral, written, and graphic discursive performances across events, times, and contexts for learning. These ways of viewing also have enlarged understanding of how discourse processes and practices, as well as language use in classrooms, supports and constrains participation and equity of access to academic institutions and to academic and social knowledge (Rex & Green, 2007).

6. Most relevant for this volume was the development of observational and analytical tools for operationalizing a situated perspective on classroom discourse. This intellectual and research work led to narrative analysis having a robust role in classroom research. Narratives could be recognized as sites of particular modes of participation involving ideologically based choices. The robustness of narrative analysis was informed by sociolinguistic and microethnographic studies that developed methods for analyzing discourse in use in classrooms. Some of these forms of analysis, explicated as narrative analysis in this volume, showed connections between local conversation and broader sociological issues, making it possible to see significant consequences of teacher and student classroom talk.

7. The scholarship of teaching and learning rests, that is, on a moral claim that I call the "pedagogical imperative." We argue that an educator can teach with integrity only if an effort is made to examine the impact of his or her work on the students. The "pedagogical imperative" includes the obligation to inquire into the consequences of one's work with students. This is an obligation that devolves on individual faculty members, programs, institutions, and even disciplinary communities (Shulman, 2002).

8. The distinction is complicated, in part, because, unlike most professions such as engineering, medicine, research, and law, educational practice does not have a uniform consensual ethical code. Individual educators, their schools, professional organizations, and accrediting institutions determine their own criteria for ethical responsibility. Consequently, a diversity of situated ethical codes exists for teachers to navigate. This condition, although allowing for local control and context relevance, has the effect of diffusing authority for inquiring into the consequences of one's work with students. This circumstance also diffuses research-based attention to issues that could inform teachers' ethical decisions. Without an agreed-on ethical code, developing research-based applicable methods for teachers' inquiry into the ethics of their practice has also been more diffuse. I do not mean to imply that a single code of ethics would improve this condition, but rather I offer one reason, among many, that research into ethical educational practice issues, and its applications in teacher education, has not been more forthcoming.

9. Steve Bodnar and Andrea Zellner are both white while 98% of their high school English students are black. They and Monica teach in the same school district and are unique among their colleagues, in that both acknowledge race

as a central focus in their teaching. Both have invited researchers into their classrooms to study their practices, and both have contributed to subsequent publications about the implications of race in literacy education and classroom research.

# REFERENCES

Bakhtin, M. M. (1981). *The dialogic imagination: Four essays by M. M. Bakhtin* (M. Holquist, Ed.; C. Emerson & M. Holquist, Trans.). Austin: University of Texas Press.

Bakhtin, M. M. (1990). *Art and answerability* (V. Liapunov & K. Brostrom, Trans.). Austin: University of Texas Press.

Bakhtin, M. M. (1993). *Toward a philosophy of the act* (V. Liapunov & M. Holquist, Eds.; V. Liapunov, Trans.). Austin: University of Texas Press.

Beers, K. (2002). *When kids can't read: What teachers can do.* Portsmouth, NH: Heinemann.

Borko, H., Cone, R., Russo, N. A., & Shavelson, R. J. (1979). Teachers' decision making. In P. Peterson & H. J. Walberg (Eds.), *Research on teaching: Concepts, findings, and implications* (pp. 136–160). Berkeley, CA: McCutchan.

Bredekamp, S. (1997). Developmentally appropriate practice: The early childhood teacher as decision maker. In S. Bredekamp & C. Copple (Eds.), *Developmentally appropriate practice in early childhood programs* (rev. ed., pp. 33–52). Washington, DC: National Association for the Education of Young Children.

Bruner, J. (1986). *Actual minds, possible worlds.* Cambridge, MA: Harvard University Press.

Bulterman-Bos, J. A. (2008). Will a clinical approach make educational research more relevant for practice? *Educational Researcher, 37*(7), 412–420.

Cochran-Smith, M., & Lytle, S. L. (2006). Troubling images of teaching in No Child Left Behind. *Harvard Educational Review, 76*, 668–697.

Connelly, F. M., & Clandinin, D. J. (1988). *Teachers as curriculum planners.* New York: Teachers College Press.

DeCuir, J., & Dixson, A. (2004). "So when it comes out, they aren't that surprised that it is there": Using critical race theory as a tool of analysis of race and racism in education. *Educational Researcher, 33*, 26–31.

Elbaz, F. (1981). The teacher's "practical knowledge": Report of a case study. *Curriculum Inquiry, 11*(1), 43–71.

Feiman-Nemser, S., & Floden, R. E. (1986). The cultures of teaching. In M. C. Wittrock (Ed.), *Handbook of research on teaching* (3rd ed., pp. 505–526). New York: Macmillan.

Foster, J. (2004). *Exploring reforms while learning to teach science: Facilitating exploration of theory and practice in a teacher education study group.* Unpublished doctoral dissertation, University of Michigan, Ann Arbor.

Geertz, C. (1973). *The interpretation of cultures.* New York: Basic Books.

Hegel, G. W. F. (1969). *Hegel's science of logic* (A. V. Miller, Trans.). New York: George Allen & Unwin.

Hegel, G. W. F. (1979). *System of ethical life (1802/1803) and first philosophy of spirit (1803–1804)* (T. M. Knox, Trans.). New York: State University of New York Press.

Hicks, D. (1991). Narrative discourse and classroom learning: An essay response to Egan's "Narrative and learning: A voyage of implications." *Linguistics and Education, 5*(2), 127–148.

Hymes, D. (1996). *Ethnography, linguistics, narrative inequality: Toward and understanding of voice.* Philadelphia: University of Pennsylvania Press.

Juzwik, M. M. (2004a). The dialogization of genres in teaching narrative: Toward a theory of hybridity in the study of classroom discourse. *Across the Disciplines: Interdisciplinary Perspectives on Language, Learning, and Academic Writing, 1.* Available at http://wac.colostate.edu/atd/.

Juzwik, M. M. (2004b). What rhetoric can contribute to an ethnopoetics of narrative performance in teaching: The significance of parallelism in one teacher's narrative. *Linguistics and Education, 15*(4), 359–386.

Juzwik, M. M. (2004c). Towards an ethics of answerability: Reconsidering dialogism in sociocultural literacy studies. *College Composition and Communication, 55*(3), 536–567.

Juzwik, M. M. (2006). Performing curriculum: Building ethos through narrative in pedagogical discourse. *Teachers College Record, 108*(4), 489–528.

Juzwik, M. M. (2009). *The rhetoric of teaching: Performing Holocaust narratives in a literacy classroom.* Cresskill, NJ: Hampton Press.

Juzwik, M. M., Nystrand, M., Kelly, S., & Sherry, M. B. (2008). Oral narrative genres as dialogic resources for classroom literature study: A contextualized case study of conversational narrative discussion. *American Educational Research Journal, 45*(4), 1111–1154.

Labov, W. (1972). *Language in the inner city: Studies in Black English vernacular.* Philadelphia: University of Pennsylvania Press.

Labov, W., & Waletsky, J. (1967). Narrative analysis: Oral versions of personal experience. In J. Helms (Ed.), *Essays on the verbal and visual arts* (pp. 12–44). Seattle: University of Washington Press.

Ladson-Billings, G. (1995). Toward a theory of culturally relevant pedagogy. *American Educational Research Journal, 32,* 465–491.

Linde, C. (1993). *Life stories: The creation of coherence.* New York: Oxford University Press.

Lipsky, M. (1980). *Street level bureaucracy: Dilemmas of the individual in public services.* New York: Russell Sage Foundation.

Marsh, M. M. (2002). The shaping of Ms. Nicholi: The discursive fashioning of teacher identities. *International Journal of Qualitative Studies in Education, 15*(3), 333–347.

Martinez-Roldan, C. (2003). Building worlds and identities: A case study of the role of narratives in bilingual literature discussions. *Research in the Teaching of English, 37,* 491–526.

Ochs, E., & Capps, L. (2001). *Living narrative: Creating lives in everyday storytelling.* Cambridge, MA: Harvard University Press.

Polanyi, L. (1985). *Telling the American story: A structural and cultural analysis of conversational storytelling.* Cambridge, MA: MIT Press.

Poveda, D. (2002). Quico's story: An ethnopoetic analysis of a Gypsy boy's narratives at school. *Text, 22*(2), 269–300.

Poveda, D. (2003). Literature socialization in a kindergarten classroom. *Journal of Folklore Research, 40*(3), 233–272.

Rex, L. A. (2000). Judy constructs a genuine question: A case for interactional inclusion. *Teaching and Teacher Education, 16*, 315–333.

Rex, L. A. (2001). The remaking of a high school reader. *Reading Research Quarterly, 36*, 288–314.

Rex, L. A. (2003). Loss of the creature: The obscuring of inclusivity. *Communication Education, 52*(1), 30–46.

Rex, L. A. (2006a). Acting "cool" and "appropriate": Toward a framework for considering literacy classroom interactions when race is a factor. *Journal of Literacy Research, 38*(3), 275–325.

Rex, L. A. (Ed.). (2006b). *Discourse of opportunity, How talk in learning situations creates and constrains.* Cresskill, NJ: Hampton Press.

Rex, L. A., & Green, J. L. (2007). Classroom discourse and interaction: Reading across the traditions. In *International Handbook of Educational Linguistics* (pp. 571–584). London: Blackwell.

Rex, L. A., & McEachen, D. (1999). If anything is odd, inappropriate, confusing or boring, it's probably important: The emergence of inclusive academic literacy through English classroom discussion practices. *Research in the Teaching of English, 34*, 66–130.

Rex, L. A., Murnen, T., Hobbs, J., & McEachen, D. (2002). Teachers' pedagogical stories and the shaping of classroom participation: "The Dancer" and "Graveyard Shift at the 7-11." *American Educational Research Journal, 39*, 765–796.

Shulman, L. S. (2002). Foreword. In P. Hutchins (Ed.), *Ethics of inquiry: Issues in the scholarship of teaching and learning.* Stanford, CA: Carnegie Foundation.

Spillane, J.P. (2004). *Standards deviation: How schools misunderstand education policy.* Cambridge, MA: Harvard University Press.

Shavelson, R. J., & Stern, P. (1981). Research on teachers' pedagogical thoughts, judgments, decisions, and behavior. *Review of Educational Research, 51*, 455–498.

White, H. (1981). The value of narrativity in the representation of reality. In J. T. Mitchell (Ed.), *On narrative* (pp. 1–24). Chicago: University of Chicago Press.

Wortham, S. (2001). *Narratives in action: A strategy for research and analysis.* New York: Teachers College Press.

# 2

# A TEACHER-PRACTITIONER'S PERSPECTIVE ON NARRATION

## *Stephen Bodnar*

"Mr. Bodnar, who's that broad?"

We had been reading Shakespeare's *Othello* for several days out loud in class, had gone over the characters, and had, in fact, been discussing Othello and his wife, Desdemona, only the day before when Jasmine asked her question. If she didn't know who she was, others probably didn't either. I thought, don't these kids read? Don't they pay attention? "Well," I said, impatiently, "Desdemona is Othello's wife and . . ."

I mention this exchange because I'm reminded, after reading the chapters in this book, how classroom teachers see *narration* almost solely as a literary assignment "to teach" ("Read chapter I, scenes ii and iii for tomorrow"), isolated facts to remember ("Desdemona is Othello's wife"), or a rhetorical mode to write in ("Write about a time when you were jealous"). What we don't realize, perhaps because it was never learned in the first place, is that classroom teachers can go beyond this interpretation, however pedagogically sound it is. Narration, as Lesley Rex points out in her Introduction, can be used in the classroom as a linguistic tool for something deeper, more vital: not for change—but for what I think of as *transformation*. Change, after all, can be good or bad; often, it's ephemeral. But transformation is *always* good, and it lasts.

A baseball friend of mine who teaches at the University of Michigan–Dearborn once said to me, as we were driving to Toledo on a sunny day to see the Mud Hens play, that all writing has some argumentation in it. I thought, hmm, you're right. But only after years of teaching in the public school system have I come to see the flip side, and it's equally as important. Robert Frost said that there's really only one meter in poetry: iamb. The others are merely a variation of it. The same can be said for narration: The other rhetorical modes—such as description, classification, comparison, and even argumentation—are all variations of the narrative because all of them have a part of our story in them or at least the seed of a story, if not in the writing itself, then certainly in the *verbal* story behind the writing, the story of how it's written, or, more precisely, the story of how we believe it came to be written.

As such, sometimes I think my classroom is one big story: stories connected to bits of stories connected to more stories like the long and winding peel of an apple. We hear these stories every day from our students, often when they fail to turn in an assignment: "I *had* my paper written and everything and I *wanted* to print it out but my printer wouldn't work and then I tried my father's printer and that wouldn't work so I saved it and e-mailed it to you in a file because I didn't want it to be late, I know how you hate late papers, and, ah . . . would you mind printing it out for me?"

But how many of these stories do we really hear? And, if we hear them, how many do we care about? How many transform our students? How many transform us?

Early in my secondary teaching career, I taught an honors Jr. Comp/Lit class. We were reading *The Great Gatsby*. To make the story more real, more tangible, I brought in some artifacts from the period, things my mother saved from my late grandmother who must have been in her 20s in the 1920s: a hair brush, a carved wooden picture frame (my grandfather carved it) with my grandmother's young portrait in it, jewelry, letters. I played music from the period, showed some baseball pictures from the 1919 Black Sox World Series. I passed around my grandmother's picture; the students delicately held the wooden frame, ran their fingers lightly over the old varnished wood, their mouths slightly open. I told stories about my grandmother, about the Black Sox scandal, about life in the Roaring Twenties. Students stared at the artifacts, listened to the stories, asked questions, told their own stories about their grandmothers, and were, in short, interested, engaged. Then we talked, *really talked*, about Gatsby.

My principal at the time, a well-meaning man who genuinely had the students' intellectual interest at heart, happened to be sitting in my classroom taking all of this in. After the lesson, he came up to me and said, "Those students are going to remember that lesson for a long time. But I want to ask you a question: What does any of this have to do with the MEAP?" (MEAP—the Michigan Educational Assessment Plan—was Michigan's version of the yearly high-stakes test administered to juniors to assess educational progress. It was dropped last year in favor of a version of the ACT.) I sort of fumbled around for something to say as he looked at me somewhat sympathetically, and I realized his question wasn't meant to be answered. The implication was clear: These *stories* aren't rigorous academics, so if you're going to tell them, tell them quickly and move on to something that *does* have something to do with the MEAP.

Today, high-stakes tests tend to drive the curriculum. The appeal is to the mind, the intellect. But narration appeals to the heart, the emotions: the affect. As pedagogical research has shown time and time again, it's affect that drives cognition. Stories touch us, move us. Jeremy Hsu (2008), writing in *Scientific American Mind*, says, ". . . stories have a unique power to persuade and motivate, because they appeal to our emotions and capacity for empathy" (p. 46). We all like a good story. Especially teachers.

Unfortunately, at times, I find myself all too often telling *un*true stories to myself about my students. And I have no hesitation, as Mary Juzwik says, to take a moral stance when something goes wrong. I'm right. The students? Why, they're wrong, of course. When they don't do their work, it's because they don't care or they're lazy. When a parent doesn't show up for a parent–teacher conference, it's because they're not interested in their son or daughter's academics. Almost always, however, these stories are wrong. I had Robert in a class last year, and I have him again this year. He failed last year, and he's struggling again this year. Obviously his mother doesn't care; after all, I've never heard from her. Last week, she sent me an impassioned e-mail asking me to keep her posted on his progress. So much for the uncaring mother. Michael, a very good student, began slacking off in his assignments. My story? He got complacent, self-satisfied, and stopped trying. Then I found out that his mother had died. It coincided with when he stopped trying. Alexandria stopped doing her work suddenly. It was late April, and I assumed she had "senioritis," a common malady that spreads across the country like dandelions in the spring. But one day she came to me in tears and told me the whole story. She wouldn't be able to go to the college of her choice because her family couldn't afford it. It wasn't that she didn't care but that she cared *too much*. The list could go on.

I'm happy that the chapters in this book emphasize, in part, the importance in teacher education of being aware of the stories we tell our students and, by implication, the stories we tell *about* our students to ourselves. So much grief can be avoided.

Several years ago, I had a student named Curtis in my creative writing class. He was a tough, street-wise kid who played football. He wasn't much interested in poetry (again, my story) and sat in back. He went through the motions when writing. He slept a little and talked a lot to those around him. I became frustrated. We had a running feud for a good part of the semester. I'd castigate him; he'd roll his eyes, talk under his breath. He'd say, "You don't know me." But I did. He was a slacker, a troublemaker. He'd say that he didn't want to do this stuff. I'd say if you didn't, you'd fail. But nothing I said made a difference. I knew one thing, though. It couldn't go on this way. I had to do something.

The "something" I did—out of exasperation, maybe desperation— was to drop the untrue story about him that I was clinging to. After all, I didn't know who Curtis was. All I really knew was that he wasn't doing his work and he was arguing with me. The rest—"he's a slacker, a trou- blemaker," attributes attributable to his attitude and mental makeup— was a story I simply made up to make me feel better about myself by blaming him for the breakdown in communication. It also, conveniently, absolved me from looking closer at the integrity of my teaching and kept the illusion that I was keeping firm control of the class.

One day before class began I called Curtis into the hallway and said I needed to talk to him. He slowly, almost painfully, got out of his seat and began walking to the door, shaking his head the whole time as if to say, "Another talk? What's the use?" Once outside, I said, "Curtis, I'm sorry. I want to apologize for not listening to you, not listening to what you were trying to tell me. I promise that from here to the end of the semester, I will listen to you. Okay?" It was probably the first time a teacher had ever apologized to him, possibly the first time an adult had ever apologized to him. In that instant, I believe, he dropped his own story about me, the one that said I was insensitive, uncaring. And this tough kid looked me in the eyes (for the first time) and said, "Mr. Bodnar, I want to apologize to you, too." Stephanie Kerschbaum labels these moments "opportunistically open" opportunities to engage students in ways meaningful to them and us. Dropping my moral stance and accept- ing Curtis' differences not only transformed my relationship with Curtis, but it transformed my class. I saw my students as more than faces, more even than individuals. I saw myself *in them*.

I can't say that Curtis was a model student from that point on, but his classroom production increased significantly, and he wrote two poems for a fundraiser called "Poetry That Heals," an event to pay for a col- league's medical bills after he was paralyzed in a sledding accident. His reading drew enthusiastic applause from the large audience, and he was clearly pleased. His eyes met mine and he nodded to me, almost imper- ceptibly, as he left the mike. It was a nod that spoke volumes. It was a nod that told a story of his life—and mine.

Sometimes I think my classroom is one big story, stories connected to bits of stories connected to more stories. We tell the stories and we are the stories, and we are transformed into the characters within our stories. That's something Shakespeare knew. And now that we're on the subject, if I could go back to that day long ago, I'd answer Jasmine's question dif- ferently. I'd say, "Desdemona? Why . . . she's *you*. Desdemona is you."

Questions for Reflection:

1. Is transformation different from change? Is transformation possible? If you think it is, what would constitute transformed teachers, students, and classrooms?
2. Do you also assume that "really talking" is distinct from the talk that usually goes on in classrooms? If so, how would one describe it? If not, why not?
3. How do Steve Bodnar's references to narrative reflect a literary framework common in his English subject matter discipline? Do you have a working framework or definition when you think about narrative? If so, what is it?
4. What would you describe as Steve's view of being a good and proper teacher as represented in his narration about his moral stance in relation to his students' behavior? Where in his text do you see evidence for your answer? Why could this knowledge be important? How might you use Steve's narrative to generate a discussion about the ethics of teaching with your students?
5. Do you think Steve's references to his stories about students as "*un*true" or "wrong" imply some kind of "right" way to narrate students' lives and identities? If so, what would this "right" way look like? How is this right/wrong perspective useful and limiting in talking with teachers about how they narrate their students?

## REFERENCE

Hsu, J. (2008). The secrets of storytelling. *Scientific American Mind*, *19*(4), 46–51.

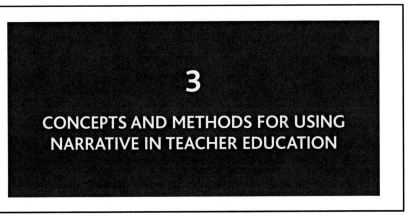

# 3
# CONCEPTS AND METHODS FOR USING NARRATIVE IN TEACHER EDUCATION

*Betsy Rymes*

*Stanton Wortham*

Someone tells you a story. It seems wrong. It misrepresents someone you care about. But it has been told by someone you do not want to offend or contradict. What do you do? You feel you must say something—set the record straight, absolve your friend, clarify your relationship to her, assert your view on what is right and wrong. How do stories provoke this sense of urgency? When a story is told and interpreted, nothing less than truth, power, morality, and individual agency can be at stake, and these stakes are too high to ignore. The stories analyzed in this book illustrate that narratives bring into play those elements that bring meaning to life:

Truth: Stories can be accurate or inaccurate. But even inaccurate stories may be taken up and used as "fact."

Power: How stories are interpreted may have just as much to do with the power of those telling and listening to them as with their factual content.

Morality: The way stories are told and interpreted are always positioning tellers and audiences within a moral framework: Characters are "good" or "bad." How we tell stories and react to them positions us as "good" or "bad" people.

Individual
Agency:    How stories are told and interpreted can affect others'
           beliefs and actions.

When we understand the social, interactional, and linguistic layers
involved in the telling and interpretation of any narrative, we can harness
the force of narrative to learn about and influence our lives and the lives
of others.

Because storytelling is such a common and powerful means to
understand and relate to students and colleagues, as well as understand and take action oneself, narrative is critical to the practice of
teaching. This book is about the insights and opportunities for action
that narrative can bring. The teacher and student stories analyzed in
this volume illustrate key issues that surround the telling of any story.
Our goal in this chapter is to introduce concepts and methods used in
the rest of the book. We build on the research history provided in the
first chapter, drawing on literature from sociolinguistics, applied linguistics, psychology, and linguistic anthropology to introduce the
methods that subsequent chapters use. These methods of narrative
analysis can help educators to learn about themselves and others and to
act more effectively.

In what follows, we conceptualize the role of truth, power, morality,
and individual agency, and we outline methods for empirically studying
these critical elements that are in play in any narrating event.

## TRUTH: NEGOTIATING TRUTH
## THROUGH NARRATIVE POETICS AND PERFORMANCE

At first, it seems as if "truth" or factual accuracy would be the most
important criterion for determining whether a story told is a good one.
If a story tells the truth about something, then it is fair. If it does not, it
is not. Truth in narrative is not just about factual accuracy, however.
Narratives do not transparently represent the world but instead select
from among many potentially relevant facts and craft them into a
coherent whole. Spoken narratives are also performed, and the character of the performance influences the effects a story will have on an
audience (Baumann & Briggs, 1990). Truth is poetically crafted in every
story and negotiated within every act of storytelling. We need to
explore not only whether a story tells the truth (i.e., whether it contains
verifiable facts) but also how narrators construct and perform their stories to create truths about how we should understand and act toward
others.

## Poetics: Constructing a Narrated Event

How is truth poetically constructed in a narrative? Consider a story you've heard that contains claims you don't believe are true. It tells about, for example, a time when your friend made a potentially disrespectful remark like, "This school is a nightmare!" What made this statement count as "offensive" within the story? This may be less a matter of whether your friend actually uttered the words in question and more a matter of how they are interpreted—more a matter of "narrative truth" and less a matter of "historical truth" (Bruner, 1999). "She couldn't have meant it that way!" is a much different response than "She never said that!" A tape recording could easily prove whether your friend did or did not utter certain words. But how can we ever know what she "meant"? Presenting what someone "meant" in a story is a matter of selecting bits of context that shape how her statements are understood (Ochs & Capps, 2001; Wortham, 2001). Narrative analysis encourages us to look, as authors within this volume do, at how storytellers' poetic arrangement of narrative chunks sets up relationships within a story and how, through these relationships, a particular stance toward events and characters emerges. Your friend may come off looking bad not just because the narrator reported something she said but also because the narrator arranged the story to communicate that her utterance was bad. This volume provides some accessible tools for exploring the poetic arrangement of stories and uncovering the tacit evaluations that narrators make.

## Performance: Emergent Truth in a Narrating Event

A story does more than *represent* an event, however. Stories are also *performed* in conversation. In other words, the events of a story are always described within a narrating event that takes place between the narrator and audience (Wortham, 2001, 2006). A story not only sets up discourse-internal poetic relationships, as it describes and evaluates a narrat*ed* event, it also has performative effects within a narrat*ing* event, as the narrator tries to accomplish something with the storytelling and the audience reacts to that attempt. When you hear a story about your friend, for example, you are engaged in a narrating event, an interaction with someone who could be challenging you to defend your friend, attempting to bond with you, or just sharing a relaxing moment after a stressful day. In telling and reacting to this story, the narrator and audience work together to create a kind of truth—a lived reality about how people would interpret and react to a situation or a character. This kind of truth often resonates much more with an audience than a truth backed up with facts and figures. Paradoxically, storytellers can often construct a sense of their own truthfulness by *not* explicitly backing up their claims. By not explicitly backing up claims but instead poetically crafting and performing narratives that make claims about people, storytellers can be even more convincing than if they inserted factual footnotes at every turn (Fox, 2001). In conversational storytelling events, truth and believability are emergent qualities agreed on collectively as a story unfolds.

Through poetics and performance, narrators and their audiences construct often-shared accounts of what happened, how we should evaluate what happened, and what kinds of people the characters must have been to have acted like that. Another kind of truth that can emerge in storytelling involves the relative positions of the people who are listening to the story. Within a conversation that includes storytelling (a "narrating event"), a story and reactions to the story position audience members with respect to the kinds of characters and issues raised in the story (the "narrated event"). As the story about your friend unfolds, for example, you have choices about how to react. How you react could be transferred onto the relationships within the story being told. If your friend's remark ("This school is a nightmare!") is presented as offensive in the narrated event, by aligning with your friend in the narrating event, you are potentially positioned as offensive too. Those who align with the story's theme are positioned as good people, who all recognize this comment as problematic. Those who contest this perspective may be positioned as bad people. In this way, the narrative truth represented in the narrated event could become a lived truth in the narrating event. Thus, a story is never "just" a story. It is a story that could have lived consequences in the here and now of its telling, perhaps long after the story has been told.

## Narrative and Difference

Narrative truth is not always agreed on in practice. One reason for this is that people bring different experiences and perspectives to any story. Depending on the background of participants in a storytelling event, our perspectives will be more or less closely aligned. Because of this alignment, or lack thereof, a story can strike some listeners as accurate, well crafted, and good, but others may see it as an unjust misrepresentation. We select different features and combine them to make different points, to foreground certain features and background others. We craft stories differently, hear them differently, and thus can potentially be positioned differently by different storytelling events.

Narratives and the resources used to convey positions within them are thus what the sociolinguist Jan Blommaert (2005) calls "placed resources," the meaning of which depends on the positions of the people participating in the narrating event. If we are in a situation in which all people are likely to agree with us, our narratives are likely to be effective.

But if we are surrounded by different kinds of people, the story may never get off the ground. How can we know the relevant presuppositions that go into understanding a narrative? How do we know how narrative presuppositions "place" or position us in a given storytelling event? In addition to looking at the text of a narrative, we need to look at the cultural backgrounds and varying beliefs among relevant subgroups in our context. This background information can suggest why individuals tell and react to stories in various ways.

This volume analyzes narrating as one important site in which teachers and students do cognitive, ethical, and interpersonal work. Narratives, because of the various truths represented in them, both carry traces of our differences and provide a medium for the negotiation of those differences. This use of narrative to understand the depth of our differences—the extent to which we all see "truth" differently—arises in all the chapters in this volume. Juzwik raises the question, for example, of how a teacher's narrative depiction of the Holocaust positions a student whose relative was a Nazi soldier. How can truth be represented in a way that redeems this student's family member (and the student participating in the class discussion)? Kerschbaum analyzes how two undergraduates position each other through stories about their dramatically different high school experiences in a relatively privileged and a relatively underprivileged school. How can those chasms in experience be represented in a way that explains and justifies the current peer-to-peer relationship between these two students? Johnson looks at how a teacher candidate's story can be interpreted as both evidence of a pre-service teacher's sense of entitlement and a critique of the elitist structure of higher education.

Each of these analyses raises questions not only about whether the educational stories are accurate—although truth is often an important and contested issue, one that is especially evident in narratives about the Holocaust—but also about how the stories are poetically crafted to do the cognitive, ethical, and interpersonal work of understanding and identifying oneself and others. These analyses are about truths that emerge within storytelling events for people in particular contexts and for particular purposes. Each of the authors emphasizes that, by attending to the poetics and performance of these occasions and by analyzing the diverse narrative voices among teachers and students and within teacher education, we may be able to contribute to the fashioning of new truths that serve teachers and students better.

## Methods for Uncovering Narrative Truth

To understand what narratives have to tell us about diversity and other aspects of teaching and learning, we need a set of tools for understanding both the poetic organization of a story and the performative effects of that story. Traditional analyses of narrative focused primarily on the structure of the narrative and built on a framework for narrative set forth by Labov and Waletsky (1967/1997). Following the idea of a literary narrative that includes recognizable elements, Labov proposed a six-component standard form for oral narratives: Abstract, Orientation, Evaluation, Complication, Resolution, and a Coda (this account is described in more detail in Chapter 4). In this book, you will see that most narrative analyses start with some sort of narrative chunking of this type. This type of pattern can become a tool for crafting a consistent narrative truth. A narrative "resolution" that involves punching someone in "self-defense," for example, only makes sense when framed by an orientation, evaluation, and complication that begs to be resolved with such a rash action. Within the standard expectations of this form, truth—the truth that self-defense was necessary, for example—is judged on the basis of the interconnectedness of these parts. As we analyze a narrative form such as this, it becomes clear that the relationship between, say, the orientation section (or "setting") of a story and the evaluation or complications within a story can make it seem that certain courses of action are more appropriate than others (Capps & Ochs, 1997). In this sense, we can examine the chunks of a narrative to explore how a narrator is constructing a coherent narrative truth.

Regardless of how careful a narrator is in crafting the story internally (e.g., of linking an orientation to a complication), effective narrators must also simultaneously monitor and account for an audience's reactions. That is why analyzing oral narratives is not simply a matter of structural or grammatical analysis but also a matter of *discourse* analysis. What methods do we use to understand how narratives unfold in interaction? Instead of specifying a normative linear structure, a specific slot for a dramatic event, or a specific slot for a conclusion, Ochs and Capps argue in their wide-ranging treatise on conversational narrative, *Living Narrative* (2001), that it is more fruitful to analyze oral narratives in terms of the degree to which stories attend to different dimensions that unfold during a story's telling:

Tellership: who is telling the story;

Tellability: how interesting the story is;

Embeddedness: how the story is situated within a stretch of talk;

Linearity: the sequential or temporal ordering of events; and

Moral Stance: the moral values being conveyed through the telling.

These dimensions are highly variable across narratives. The dimensions of "tellability" and "tellership," in particular, highlight the part of narrative analysis that attends to its performance in an interaction. Some facts universally strike us as highly "tellable." A murder or an act of adultery, for example, is a fact that, in and of itself, renders a story exciting. But a storyteller who is attuned to her audience can make nearly anything tellable by noticing how an audience responds to story details and making narrative choices accordingly as the story unfolds. In this way, an audience, even by their simple physical presence, acts as a co-teller of any story. Thus, reporting someone who said "This school is a nightmare!" might be made into an entertaining story—a tellable oral narrative—by the way the storyteller frames that comment both within structural expectations for a narrative and in terms of the audience she is addressing. Therefore, tellability and (co-)tellership are tightly linked dimensions of storytelling that are highly contingent not only on the facts and structural expectations that feed the narrated event but also on the relationships that are in play during the narrating event.

Discourse analysts have tools for investigating the co-tellership and tellability of a narrative. How do story recipients respond to the storyteller's setup? What a storyteller means can only be accomplished if listeners agree, during the course of the telling, to that meaning. Depending on how listeners respond, "This school is a nightmare!" could take on any number of functions: a joke, a complaint, an act of blatant disrespect or negligence, a cry for help, a politically rallying cry, and so on. Part of what that comment means can be analyzed by its situation within a story's structure. But whether listeners laugh, frown, or get up and storm out of the room will also shape how that story unfolds, what that comment really meant, and what it will mean in the future (Ochs, 1994). These reactions also determine whether a remark subsequently counts as "tellable" or mundane.

The kind of truth that emerges in a storytelling event—the lived reality that follows a narrating event—can be analyzed by attending carefully to the story structure and the way in which story elements are reacted to in the narrating event. As the narratives analyzed in the following chapters illustrate, identifying a story's structure can be a starting point for an analysis. Identifying how that structure is shaped by the others present within a narrative performance is a necessary next step. By attending to the tension between narrative structure and narrative performance, these analyses attend to emergent truths that affect the people telling, listening, and being told about.

## POWER: THE NATURALIZATION OF CONVENTION THROUGH NARRATIVE POETICS AND PERFORMANCE

Once we recognize that narrative truth, although oriented to verifiable facts, is also emergent within the storytelling event, we cannot ignore the possibility that some people's versions of the truth may take precedence.

There are not only multiple versions of the truth, but some of these versions normally count more than others. Our narrative resources are not only "placed" or socially positioned, but they are also differentially valued. Within a narrating event, some ways of telling a story may seem intuitively more "natural" than others. Why is this?

Sometimes certain perspectives come to seem "natural" because people in higher positions in a structural hierarchy hold them. Other interpretations seem "marginal" because people in marginal structural slots hold them. Narrative can reinforce the power of dominant points of view if powerful people deploy their points of view in telling and reacting to narratives. Moreover, discourse-internal features of narratives can carry those dominant views from interaction to interaction. Parmentier (1994) calls this the "naturalization of convention."

However, narrative performances also provide some degree of wiggle room—no story is told in a vacuum, and when alternative perspectives are voiced, there is a possibility to contest even the most structurally embedded, "naturalized" perspectives. Chapters in this volume analyze the structural, discourse-internal language of narrative and also the performative effects of those narratives in an encounter to expose the workings—and sometimes the undoing—of this "naturalization" process.

## Discourse-Internal Power

How do linguistic resources make conventions seem "natural?" Narratives are only one mechanism through which people accomplish naturalization, but they can be powerful ones. Within a narrative, relationships between words and the sounds that compose words gain power by constructing more or less repeatable chunks of language. These repeatable chunks come to represent natural-seeming perspectives. Think, for example, of a poetically repeatable phrase from Martin Luther King's "I Have a Dream" speech, his hope for the day when children will "be judged by the content of their character and not the color of their skin." This fragment is resonant, in part, because of the simple alliteration between the words "content," "character," and "color." This similitude renders the fragment repeatable, and so it becomes memorable apart from the context in which it is told. In the same way, the repeated parallel iterations of "I have a dream..." in King's speech, just like Shakespeare's "To be or not to be" or the Bible's "Thou shalt not..." have turned these collections of words into memorable bits that stand on their own. This kind of speech is easily extractable from its context, and thus it can circulate widely and have the power to influence how people think about things (Baumann & Briggs, 1990).

Once something is extractable, it can be more easily placed into new contexts (like other narratives). "I have a dream" is not only a memorable phrase, but it is also one that has been used and reused in interaction after interaction ever since Martin Luther King, Jr. first spoke those words. So, paradoxically, discourse-internal features of language such as alliteration or poetic repetition can facilitate the traveling of a text and its message beyond the initial setting of its occurrence—making that message endure as something more "natural," not simply an isolated feature of one speech event that arises from a particular perspective. Well-crafted narratives, just like isolated phrases within them, can become powerful beyond the immediate context of their occurrence, in part, because of their discourse-internal structure. Such narratives are "powerful" because they naturalize the storylines they convey. This recognizable combination of features, deployed within narrative, may subsequently travel beyond narrating events. Moreover, these poetic, recontextualized chunks may have existed long before singular narrating events as a part of some preexistent, allegedly "natural" discourse ("Thou shalt not...").

## Performative Power

The structural features of words and their conventionally understood meanings combine to create such discourse-internal effects. In performance, those effects can be taken up in normative or non-normative ways. In King's speech, for example, he not only makes great use of language, but he also makes great *re*-use of language, taking entextualized bits from the past and reperforming them for new effects during his speech. From the Declaration of Independence, he takes, "We hold these truths to be self-evident, that all men are created equal," and he recontextualizes this recognizable bit in a way that resonates anew, in the context of the civil rights movement. When King pronounces "that *all* men are created equal," he draws on the lasting power of the original declaration, and he brings it into service of the current performance—a black man demanding that this sentiment be honored (Urban, 2001).

Narratives are powerful because they have memorable discourse-internal structures such as repetition of various sorts and because we can extract those memorable "truths" from specific narratives and re-perform those bits to achieve new effects. Just as the "truth" of a story emerges in the tension between discourse-internal poetics and performative aspects of narrative, so a narrative's effective "power" emerges within a narrating event through the combination of discourse-internal relationships (such as the memorable clause penned by the founding fathers, "All men are created equal") with the emerging relationships between audience members and the storyteller in the narrating event (such as reminder by Martin Luther King, Jr., that "*All* men are created equal"). King told stories and used other genres in a way that overcame previously entrenched, powerful belief systems by skillfully redeploying linguistic resources in new contexts.

## Reproducing and Inverting Power Hierarchies Through Narrative Poetics and Performance

But how powerful can narrative form and performance be relative to the social hierarchies that are present in any storytelling event? Richard Parmentier (1994) observed that, in some social contexts, "power might be best viewed as the harnessing of forces through innovative semiotic tropes rather than as the manipulation of cultural conventions by differentiated social hierarchies" (p. 124). This suggests that, counter to typical worries about necessary silence in the face of higher-ups, innovative semiotic tropes (such as a well-crafted counterstory or King's recycling of "*All* men are created equal") could redress an offensive situation while minimizing risk. It could be that a well-told counternarrative or rebuttal could have an effect despite preexisting hierarchies.

The power of language may in fact sometimes be more powerful than the power of the entrenched social hierarchy. The narrative analyses within this volume begin to illustrate how narrative force can in some cases be harnessed to contend with seemingly intractable social hierarchies and differences. The chapters in this volume all illustrate how certain features of a story may become entextualized in powerful ways, taken up and reperformed to great effect. Taken as a group, these chapters also suggest how social hierarchies variably influence the performative effects of narratives. Implied in Juzwik's chapter is consideration of the extent to which a teacher's rhetoric—especially compellingly performed narratives—can exclude student voices and perspectives. Thus, it is possible that the teacher may have so much power within the classroom that her rhetoric will inevitably dominate (cf. Juzwik, 2006). Kerschbaum's student narratives, however, illustrate how stereotypical social hierarchies can be subverted through narrative and counternarrative. Kerschbaum's analysis of two students' parallel stories about their respective experiences—at an elite private high school and a substandard public high school—illustrates how a well-placed story can flip a typical hierarchy. The contrast between the potential for reproduction of established hierarchy in Juzwik's study and the reversal in Kerschbaum's illustrates the potential for narrative analyses to address the various possible forms that individual stories can take within educational settings.

## Methods for Uncovering Rhetorical Power

To understand what narrative analysis can tell us about power and hierarchy in teacher education, we need to take up the analytic tools that uncover those uses of language that construct new relationships or reproduce old hierarchies. The power of language to craft ready-made, reproducible bits resides, in part, in the poetic ways we memorably combine linguistic forms. So our work as analysts includes deciphering the patterns of language that recur across interactions. These patterns include rhythm and rhyme but also countless other features such as alliteration, repetition, and parallelism. A memorable phrase such as King's rhythmic repetition of "I have a dream" or even the rhythmic rhyme of Johnny Cochran's "If the glove doesn't fit, we must acquit" can carry these phrases from interaction to interaction, collecting standard meanings or even reworking the meanings to create new understandings that can be memorably conveyed in a subsequent encounter. Analysis, then, involves tracking these patterned bits and their trajectories across interactions.

Poetic devices such as parallelism, rhyme, and repetition are resources for our work as discourse analysts when we look at a transcript. Moreover, when we listen to a tape or watch a video of an interaction, we can also analyze the patterns of rhythm, intonation, and stress that make certain bits of language memorable and repeatable. Think, for example, of the difference between a mumbled version of "This school is a nightmare" and a pert, smiling version: "This school is a NIGHTmare!" One version might portray a depressed, lackadaisical teacher. One might portray a spunky, funny version of a tongue-in-cheek complaint. Indeed, "This school is a nightmare!" (and its recognizable, patterned intonation) could be taken up by an entire peer group as a silly complaint, a funny refrain, a shared in-joke. The possibilities are endless. The point is that language and its delivery present us with new ways of making bits of language memorable.

In a narrating event, these memorable bits of language carry power. As narrative analysts, we can track how these bits of language are crafted and how they function within a narrative structure, but we can also track how they are taken up by a listening audience and how, in turn, they are carried forward into subsequent narratives and interactions. By looking at a transcript or videotape, we can observe "power" as a process of naturalization of convention—or as resistance to such naturalization—by analyzing whether poetically crafted bits of language are taken up by others and how. In Kerschbaum's chapter, for example, one student positions her own meager high school education in direct parallel with her peer's account of an elite private school curriculum. Rather than accounting for her experience in terms of a stereotypical lament about her lack of preparation for college, however, the public school alumnus uses the parallelism of her and her peer's accounts to create a more heroic role for herself. "I don't know how I ended up here [at this elite university], no idea, yeah, but it's worth it," she concludes. The implication, through the parallel, is that her rise to the university was much more impressive given her background. Through the parallelism, she avoids a possible alternative reading of her trajectory—that she is a lowly individual who will probably not do well at university because she has not had the advantages of a quality high school education. It may even be that, by framing her story this way, she constructs a new truth, creating a reality in which college success is more likely for her than for a peer who has taken her own education for granted. Exercising power through narration, then, becomes a matter of reproducing or reworking canonical expectations, rather than being passively subject to them. As Kerschbaum nicely illustrates, analyzing narrative involves finding these concrete poetic traces.

## MORALITY: FROM CRAFTING A MORAL TALE
## TO ANSWERING TO A MORAL HIERARCHY

Stories do more than allow narrators and audience members to establish truth and enact power. They also allow speakers and hearers to establish a shared sense of what is good and bad, right and wrong. Traditional moral tales such as fables explicitly tell us how to behave. In more subtle ways, ordinary stories can also position us within a moral hierarchy. Sometimes these tacit moral messages are communicated through aspects of the narrated story, such as the representation of morally questionable "bad guys." Sometimes moral messages are communicated through ethically salient positioning within the narrating event, as when the audience members position themselves against bad guys and their actions as they unfold in the storytelling. As Johnson writes, listening to teachers' narratives can be a way of "helping teachers learn more about themselves as moral beings." This listening requires that we understand the relationships described in the narrated content of the story and that we grapple with the moral positions that these narrated relationships can project onto the narrating event.

### Narrative as Moral Craft: Constructing a Moral Tale
### Through Narrative Particularity

A moral hierarchy arranges one morality with respect to others. Any story tacitly contains moral stances that position some moral judgments as superior to others and some characters as morally superior to others.

Within a narrative, tellers draw on various poetic devices to evoke these relative moral positions. Specific words and other linguistic devices describe and evaluate roles and behaviors, highlight certain acts as good, condemn certain actions as reprehensible, and invoke various stereotypes. But within stories, characters are not unambiguously "good" or "bad" the way electrons carry "positive" or "negative" charges. The best stories invite listeners into the world of the characters by situating actions within a detailed set of concerns. So, just as story structure can be designed to make a story believable or bits arranged to develop a story's rhetorical power, so details within a story can be fashioned in ways that create empathy and compassion and develop a nuanced moral hierarchy not necessarily based on natural or immutable laws but on the unique, situated details of the story.

As Martha Nussbaum (1995) has written, when we read a good novel or hear a good story, we are constituted as judges by that story. Our judgment, ideally, hinges on an understanding of the story details, not simply on generic versions of "good" and "bad" behavior. In other words, there are no rules detailed enough to accommodate the complexity of our daily lives. For that reason, there is always the need for aesthetic judgment. This aesthetic judgment goes into the crafting of a narrative in conversation.

The analyses in this volume illustrate in detail how storytellers construct characters, set up nuanced contrasts, or create parallels between figures from the past and figures within a narrated event. Good storytellers do not simply and straightforwardly delineate who is good, who is bad. Storytellers paint a portrait of humans behaving in the midst of a range of complex relationships and concerns. "Show, don't tell" is generic creative writing workshop advice. But it is equally applicable to the crafting of conversational narrative. "Harriet is a bad girl" is likely to be an unacceptable narrative utterance. But a careful description of a character's behavior, including quoted speech, coordinated narrative arrangement, strategic deployment of pronouns, repetition, and parallelism, may convey disdain and dismissal far more effectively. So, the aesthetics of a narrative, and judgment of a narrative's aesthetic value, is, essentially, a moral judgment. The devil (and the angel) are in the details, and respecting those details, representing them with accuracy and sense, are the means through which narrators construct a moral hierarchy within their tales.

## Narrative as Moral Performances With Consequences

Aesthetic crafting is critical. But the palpable moral force of a narrative comes from its position within a narrating event. The aesthetics of a well-wrought narrative are only morally relevant when they become "answerable" in interaction (Bakhtin, 1993). Just as a judge reaching a verdict can determine someone's life or death, when we hear a story, our decisions about the relative merits of the story's protagonist can have real consequences. The depiction of characters, the juxtaposition of these characters with respect to one another, and the placement of them within a morally charged context—all these are largely aesthetic choices distinct from the event of the story's telling. But as we have argued above, a story is never just a story

When that narrator said "This school is a nightmare," what kinds of moral lessons were at stake? What was the storyteller doing when she made the decision to tell this story, and how is her story answerable in that interaction? Obvious questions of moral responsibility emerge: Would you, by not speaking up for your own interpretation of this story, be acting inappropriately? Through the act of telling this story, the narrating event becomes a moral arena in which all individuals are answerable to the ethical issues raised in the story.

## Methods for Uncovering Narrative Morality and Its Interactional Effects

Given that moral hierarchies are essential elements of any narrative, methods for delineating those hierarchies within stories are critical to narrative analysis. As described in the previous section, features of language can become solidified into memorable bits that are loaded with expectations—expectations that can either be taken up, naturalizing certain positions, or subverted through rhetorical shifts. Kerschbaum's analysis of the parallel composition classroom stories, for example, illustrates how parallelism and careful arrangement of story chunks may be able to subvert expected hierarchies and expectations for academic achievement.

These same poetic devices that make language memorable or repeatable can also be used to situate narrative details within a moral hierarchy. Narrative details are meaningless out of context. Any single detail is impossible to place along a value hierarchy without understanding how it is situated within a broader narrative context. A narrative sets up this context, creating a moral hierarchy and situating details and people within it.

We can begin to investigate how narratives construct moral hierarchies by analyzing the arrangement of story pieces and players. Who the relevant protagonists are, what they do, and why they do it are the fundamental building blocks that construct moral hierarchies in narrative. As you look at a transcript and a recording of a narrative, then, delineate who the actors are and what actions they take. The statement "Harriet insulted Orlando," for example, includes Harriet as an agent. Her action is insulting someone. This initial departure point suggests that Harriet is a person who insults people. But what else does Harriet do in the story? Does she apologize? Bicker? Get good grades? Play sports? What does Orlando do? What people do in stories usually coalesces into a pattern of co-occurrence. Delineating these patterns can be an initial departure point for your analysis of protagonists and their positions within a storied moral hierarchy.

After accounting for who did what in a narrative, the next analytic step is to ask "why?" What rationale is presented for actions within a story? Why did Harriet insult Orlando? Is Harriet a good person despite having committed this insult? This process of understanding why actors do what they do entails the fine tuning of a moral hierarchy within a narrative. As a narrator works out what a statement such as "Harriet insulted Orlando" means, that narrator is positioning characters morally—both characters within the narrative and individuals within the narrating event. The act of insulting someone, for example, can seem wrong on the basis of generic politeness norms. But what if Harriet was simply retaliating after being insulted by Orlando for years? Maybe she was finally standing up for herself. What if Harriet and Orlando had a long relationship with a history of playful insults? These are the kinds of contingencies that create narrative particularity. As narrative analysts, we can begin to look at how these kinds of relationships are set up by analyzing subjects and predicates within narratives. Then we can extend our analysis by understanding how these acts are situated among the structure and details of a story.

Understanding these patterns and what they mean also entails a careful toggling back and forth between the implications within the narrated event ("Harriet is a bad person") and the narrating event ("I, the narrator, am the kind of person who recognizes Harriet is a bad person, which means I am morally superior to her"). Within this narrative negotiation, there are always likely to be alternative rationalizations. Although one version might frame Harriet's insult as a righteous coup after years of putting up with Orlando, another might frame it as Harriet lowering herself, stooping to Orlando's level. How those alternatives are embraced or rejected may be highly contingent on the event of telling. As storytellers simultaneously position the characters within the story, they simultaneously position themselves and their audience within a moral hierarchy.

This kind of moral positioning can occur in classrooms as teachers position themselves, through the stories they tell, as moral models for their students. The teacher in Mary Juzwik's chapter, for example, positions a student in moral limbo by decrying the acts of the Holocaust and all Hitler's minions with rhetorical aplomb. Johnson illustrates how teacher candidates and students also create moral hierarchies as they tell stories. The teacher candidate in Johnson's chapter narratively reverses her position, from being an entitled college student who expects to have technology at her fingertips to being a college student who struggles to make ends meet in the face of a university that assumes students have substantial resources available. The student in Kerschbaum's chapter also repositions her substandard high school education as an indicator of her heroic rise to success at an elite university.

Each of these examples illustrates how narrators frame their circumstances within a moral hierarchy. But these moral frames are subject to critique, and not all ways of morally framing events are equally attentive to relevant details. Once we see each of these narrative framings as one of an indefinite number of possible ways to frame events, moral positioning and the details of individual experience are available for analysis and dialogue. This raises the potential for individuals to attain positions as moral agents within stories they tell and as they interpret and participate in co-telling stories they hear.

## INDIVIDUAL AGENCY: THE POSSIBILITY
## OF TEACHER AGENCY THROUGH NARRATIVE ANALYSIS

At the beginning of this chapter, we alluded to times when we are faced with stories we sense are not accurate portrayals but that we feel unable to contest. This sense of powerlessness can be a function of structural hierarchies ("Don't bite the hand that feeds you!"). But is anyone ever really at the mercy of one interpretation, the one wielded by those higher up in a social hierarchy? We have suggested that this is not the case, that typical hierarchies can be inverted through creative use of and reactions to stories. In other words, an account of how the powerful invariably use narrative to further their own ends would misunderstand the kinds of agency that we really have in storytelling events.

Structural hierarchies, such as the power that "naturalizes" convention, do not necessarily inhibit individual freedom of action and keep us from telling powerful new stories from the margins. Instead, there are multiple varieties of agency that exist in any interaction, and the degrees of freedom granted or restricted by a social hierarchy are only one form of agency. Another critical form of agency is the ability to interpret others—in this case, to read the cognitive, ethical, and interpersonal implications of a narrative—and to understand the potential adequacy of one's response. A third, possibly most important, form of agency is one's ability to reflect on the freedom one might have to interpret and respond within a given setting (Agha, 2003, 2007). As Parmentier (1994) argues, the power to wield language in creative and nuanced ways can allow narrators and audience members to modify even entrenched social hierarchy. If we understand the various implications and constraints on our storytelling and our action, we can tell stories that might modify assumed social hierarchies rather than reinforce or naturalize them.

This book is about harnessing that ability to act as an individual agent—not simply through an act of will but by recognizing the power of interpretation and responsive dialogue that surround any narrative. In schools, teachers too often feel constrained by what they experience as normative pressures or top-down demands from an entrenched bureaucracy. Now, in a time when teachers face demands of high-stakes tests and mandated "teacher-proof" curricula, it seems that teacher agency is increasingly seen by policymakers and administrators and others as a problem rather than an important resource. Instead of being respected as thoughtful professionals, teachers are too often construed as hindrances to the efficient production of high test scores. But if we all accept this hierarchy, we simply naturalize it as inevitable. The stakes—truth, power, morality—are simply too high to acquiesce in this way. As an alternative to this stance of diminished agency, the analyses within this book illustrate that narrative and the dialogue surrounding it provide a medium in which to become more fully agentive as we engage with the world, with the field of education, and with our lived differences. Through the deployment and analysis of narrative, it becomes possible to construct new truths, negotiate our power, and become moral agents as teachers and teacher educators.

Questions for Reflection:

1. How does the discussion of narrative in this chapter resonate with, or depart from, your working understanding of narrative?
2. This chapter suggests that how stories are told and interpreted are always positioning tellers and audiences within a moral framework. Can you think of an example narrative that you have heard in a school where you have worked? Who told the story? (Teacher? Principal? Students?) Can you see any new ways that the narrative might have positioned the teller and audience within a moral framework?
3. This chapter introduces the notion of poetics and performance in relation to narrative truth. Think of a story you've heard recently. What poetic and performative resources did the teller use to construct believable truths about the world? How did you respond to this as a listener?
4. How, if at all, do you think that narrative analysis can open up possibilities for "teacher agency"? Can you think of an example in your working life as a teacher or teacher educator when narrative analysis might have been a useful tool for teacher action and advocacy? Can you think of an example where narrative analysis would *not* have been useful for teacher action and advocacy?

## REFERENCES

Agha, A. (2003). The social life of cultural value. *Language and Communication*, *23*(3–4), 231–273.

Agha, A. (2007). *Language and social relations.* New York: Cambridge University Press.

Bakhtin, M. M. (1993). *Toward a philosophy of the act* (V. Liapunor & M. Holquist, Eds.; V. Liapunov, Trans.). Austin: University of Texas Press.

Bauman, R., & Briggs, C. (1990). Poetics and performance as critical perspectives on language and social life. *Annual Review of Anthropology, 19,* 59–88.

Blommaert, J. (2005). *Discourse.* New York: Cambridge University Press.

Bruner, J. (1990). *Acts of meaning.* Cambridge, MA: Harvard University Press.

Capps, L., & Ochs, E. (1997). *Constructing panic: The discourse of agoraphobia.* Cambridge, MA: Harvard University Press.

Fox, B. (2001). Evidentiality: Authority, entitlement, and responsibility in English conversation. *Journal of Linguistic Anthropology, 11*(2), 167–192.

Juzwik, M. (2006). Performing curriculum: Building ethos through narrative in pedagogical discourse. *Teachers College Record, 108*(4), 489–528.

Labov, W., & Waletsky, J. (1967/1997). Narrative analysis: Oral versions of personal experience. *Journal of Narrative and Life History, 7*(1–4), 3–38.

Nussbaum, M. (1995). *Poetic justice: The literary imagination and public life.* Boston: Beacon Press.

Ochs, E. (1994). Stories that step into the future. In E. Biber & E. Finegan (Eds.), *Sociolinguistic perspectives on register* (pp. 106–135). New York, Oxford: Oxford University Press.

Ochs, E., & Capps, L. (2001). *Living narrative: Creating lives in everyday storytelling.* Cambridge, MA: Harvard University Press.

Parmentier, R. (1994). *Signs in society: Studies in semiotic anthropology.* Bloomington: Indiana University Press.

Urban, G. (2001). *Metaculture: How culture moves through the world.* Minneapolis: University of Minnesota Press.

Wortham, S. E. F. (2001). *Narratives in action: A strategy for research and analysis.* New York: Teachers College Press.

Wortham, S. E. F. (2006). *Learning identity: The joint emergence of social identification and academic learning.* New York: Cambridge University Press.

# 4

## UNDERSTANDING (MORAL) VIEWPOINTS THROUGH LAYERED INTERPRETATIONS OF TEACHERS' STORIES

*Amy Suzanne Johnson*

From spring 2003 to fall 2004, I conducted a study of 10 female, Euro-American, middle-class preservice elementary teachers who I had come to know as a course instructor in their teacher education program at Midwest University (pseudonym). Midwest University is well known for its commitment to preparing teachers who teach for equity and justice. I taught within the elementary undergraduate certification program as a literacy methods instructor. In this course, I focused on the rise of technology in education and the stories that the preservice teachers had to tell about emerging technologies. I pushed them to recognize technology as a sociocultural practice (e.g., Brandt, 2001; Gee, 1996; Heath, 1983; Knobel, 1999; Lankshear, 1997; New London Group, 2000; Street, 1984, 1995) that incorporated new ways of doing and engaging.

To understand how "typical" preservice teachers (Gomez, 1994) learned literacy in these "new times" and use what I learned to prepare them as future teachers, I designed a life history study that would yield insights into the social and material contexts in which they learned literacy. In initial data analyses, I learned that teachers routinely told stories in response to my seemingly closed-ended research questions: They told stories with similar *themes*, for example, how adults (either parents or teachers) struggled to find purpose in some of the newly evolving technologies that were becoming commonplace in their lives and communities. Teachers all had a story about a parent or teacher who had denied them access to the Internet or computers, who did not know how to use the Internet or computers, or who found the Internet and computers silly and unnecessary. As I studied these stories, I noticed patterns across their stories: I observed that, in using *story form*, teachers communicated a stable impression of who they were and what they believed; that teachers used similar patterns of *language and grammar* to communicate who they were and what they believed; and that narrating these stories in *interaction* with a teacher educator enabled teachers to make points about how adults can support children's literacy learning.

My curiosity with unpeeling the complexities of teachers' stories compelled me to consider how a layered analysis incorporating attention to theme, form, language, and grammar can be more firmly situated within teacher education. Such layered analysis, I suspected, held particular promise in efforts to prepare teachers who use critical reflection to better meet the needs of all learners.

In this chapter, I explore various methods that teacher educators can use for interpreting the stories teachers tell about their lives, and particularly their learning of subject matter. I explore a number of analytic angles that teacher educators can take for probing teachers' autobiographical stories, specifically focusing on theme, form, language, and interaction. In so doing, I ask:

- What can analyses of teachers' stories for each of the four layers of theme, form, language, and interaction enable teacher educators to see and hear in teachers' stories?
- How can such a layered analysis help teacher educators use narrative to prepare more critically reflective teachers?

## TEACHERS' AUTOBIOGRAPHICAL NARRATIVES

In response to the challenge of preparing teachers who are better able to meet the needs of their future students, teacher educators have brought personal, autobiographical narratives into teacher preparation programs. In so doing, they have attempted to provide teachers with opportunities to engage in sustained critical reflection on the role that their biographies play on their instructional choices, their interactions with students, and their overall outlooks on teaching, learning, schools, and society (e.g., Clandinin & Connelly, 1995, 2000; Connelly & Clandinin, 1988, 1990; Florio-Ruane, 2001; Gomez, 1994; Gomez & Abt-Perkins, 1995; Gomez & Tabachnick, 1992; Gomez, Walker, & Page, 2000; Wetherell & Noddings, 1991). Prompting such critical connections between the individual self and society is widely acknowledged as producing teachers who are more "self-actualized" (Titone, 1998) individuals and, as a result, more capable of teaching for equity. Likewise, part of urging teachers to critically connect their biographies with broader social issues is encouraging them to consider their moral perspectives and how these give shape to their instructional choices. By telling autobiographical stories in teacher education contexts, teachers can sometimes come to better understand who they are and/or who they want to be as teachers as well as what they think is "good" and "right." Sometimes, as a result of telling stories, teachers can even change who they are or what they think in a way that better supports their teaching of *all* children.

Although the "narrative turn" in teacher education has foregrounded the pedagogical potential of autobiographical narrative in cultivating a more critically reflective (Liston & Zeichner, 1991) teaching workforce, this turn has been accompanied by some tensions. For narrative work necessitates a delicate hand on the part of the teacher educator, requiring him or her to honor the teacher and her experiences while sticking to the wider purpose of bringing the teacher's experience into dialogue with broader social issues. From this perspective, teachers' narratives can sometimes seem unassailable, complicating the teacher educator's efforts to urge teachers to more critically engage with their experiences. Teacher educators need some tools that will allow them to cultivate and interpret teachers' stories in a manner that prompts critical reflection but also honors the teacher's life and experiences.

## A LAYERED APPROACH TO INTERPRETING TEACHERS' STORIES: THEME, LANGUAGE, FORM, AND INTERACTION

### The Data

I use the narrative of one participant, Lindsey Maxwell (pseudonym), to explore several approaches for interpreting teachers' stories:

*You Had to Convince Your Parents*

Amy: *Did you surf it [the Internet] at home too? Did you have it at home?*

Lindsey: I remember that was a big deal trying to get the Internet at home. Like you had to convince your parents that it was necessary to have this tool at home. It was like: "Do you understand the capabilities? Like either you spend ya know how many hundreds of dollars on like an encyclo-

pedia set." And that's what we were debating whether we
should get an encyclopedia set or the Internet. And I
remember having these conversations with my parents
and I'm like: "It's constantly updated." My dad still does-
n't regularly use the Internet. He doesn't like using it. He
doesn't understand it. Like, I remember at one point we
got it hooked up where we had some telephone system or
something on the computer. And you could call people in
different countries. And we called somebody in South
Africa. And my dad thought it was just the strangest thing
in the world that you could talk to someone in South
Africa from [state]. And we were like: "What is going on
here, ya know?" And he was having all these conversations. And I think it was at that point that he was finally
sold on the idea of having a computer and having all of
these resources that, "Hey, this could be a really cool thing
and a good learning opportunity for my kids." But trying
to get it was just….

This narrative emerged during Lindsey's life history interview when she
was prompted to respond to questions about how, where, and with
whom she learned and used literacy throughout her life span. In
recounting her at-home acquisition of technological materials deemed
necessary for her schooling, Lindsey draws on various narrative and linguistic resources to create an impression of her own sense of entitlement
toward the procurement of resources deemed essential for her literacy
learning.

## A LAYERED APPROACH
## TO NARRATIVE ANALYSIS

I examine four layers of this story: theme, form, language and grammar,
and interaction. With each of these layers are associated different analytic foci and guiding questions that I represent in four tables (Tables
4.1–4.4). These tables do not present exhaustive lists of guiding questions
a teacher educator might draw on as she interprets a teacher's story but
are merely presented as a guide for focusing one's inquiry.

When interpreting the *theme* of a teacher's story, a teacher educator
focuses analytically on the content of the story and the identity of the
teacher that such content foregrounds. To get at such analytic foci, I present guiding questions in Table 4.1.

TABLE 4.1.
Questions Pursued in a Thematic Analysis of Teachers' Narratives

| ANALYTIC FOCI | GUIDING QUESTIONS |
| --- | --- |
| Content | What does the teacher talk about? |
| | What themes emerge throughout the course of her narration? |
| | How do these themes compare to those emergent in other teachers' talk? |
| Identity | What do these themes indicate about the teacher? |
| | What do these themes suggest about the teacher's identity in relation to other teachers' identities? |

In so doing, thematic analyses can shed light on the beliefs that constitute a teacher's knowledge base (Clandinin & Connelly, 1986; McVee, 2004) and that may potentially shape her practice as a teacher).

Sociolinguistic perspectives on interpreting narratives can offer teacher educators some tools for understanding how teachers use patterned *forms* of storytelling as resources for articulating their beliefs and identities (e.g., Capps & Ochs, 1995; Gee, 1985, 1986, 1991; Labov, 1972; Labov & Waletzky, 1967/1997; Schiffrin, 1994). According to Labov and Waletzky (1967/1997), stories include the following components:

Abstract: *The synopsis of what the story is about.*
Orientation: *The temporal, spatial, and/or psychological setting for the events.*
Evaluation: *The point of the story.*
Complications: *The predicament on which the narrative is focused.*
Resolution: *The solving of the problem or the effects of the predicament.*
Coda: *The signal that the story has ended.*

Looking at a story's structure is important because how a teacher structures her story—what she chooses to emphasize and omit, her stance as protagonist or victim, and the relationship the story establishes between herself and her audience —all shape what a teacher can claim about her life (Rosenwald & Ochberg, 1992). When interpreting the form of a teacher's story, a teacher educator might focus analytically on the structure of a story and on what this structure reveals about a teacher's identity (see Table 4.2).

TABLE 4.2.
Questions Pursued in a Formal Analysis of Teachers' Narratives

| ANALYTIC FOCI | GUIDING QUESTIONS |
| --- | --- |
| *Structure* | Does the teacher's narrative have an identifiable form? If so, what is it? |
| | How does the teacher draw on this form as a means for organizing her talk and articulating themes? |
| *Identity* | What do these themes and storylines indicate about the teacher? |
| | What does her use of narrative structure indicate about the teacher? |

Yet if our aim as teacher educators is to provide aspiring teachers with tools for sustaining critical inquiry as a means to enact and sustain reflection beyond their initial teacher education experiences, then we must consider the rudimentary tools of *language* used to construct a teacher's beliefs and identities. An unexpressed aim of teacher education is to recruit pre- and in-service teachers into a discourse community where teaching, learning, education, students, families, and communities are talked about using certain kinds of language and grammar. An important goal of teacher storytelling within teacher education contexts, then, should be for teachers to better understand their "communicative palettes" (Capps & Ochs, 1995, p. 179). Inquiry into one's communicative palettes is necessary within teacher education, so that teachers can recognize and identify the ethical "hues and textures rendered by particular linguistic forms" (Capps & Ochs, 1995, p. 179)—namely, those that condemn and those that condone multiple ways of being in the world. In repeatedly considering how they use language to package experience into narrative form, teachers may become more reflective on their language choices and how these can come together to shape reality. When analyzing the language and grammar of a teacher's story, a teacher educator might start by focusing analytically on verbs of saying, verb tense or aspect, and dialogue between characters (see Table 4.3).

Finally, when telling stories, a teacher acts like a certain kind of person and *interactionally* enacts a certain kind of social position for herself and her audience (cf. Wortham, 2001). Each social position is associated with viewpoints, stances, and ways of being. The same can be said for each social position that teachers attribute to other individuals and their audiences. As teachers speak to, about, and for others, they cast these individuals as certain kinds of people who see the world in certain ways. Moreover, these different social positions are associated with different interactional contexts, which also contribute to the viewpoints and

TABLE 4.3.
Questions Pursued in a Linguistic
and Grammatical Analysis of Teachers' Narratives

| ANALYTIC FOCI | GUIDING QUESTIONS |
| --- | --- |
| *Verbs of Saying* | What words does the teacher use to describe the speech of herself and others? How does this word choice shape the characterization of herself and others? |
| *Verb tense* | What verb tense does the teacher use to recount past events? How does this choice in verb tense contribute to the overall feel of the story and its events? |
| *Dialogue* | What tone of voice does the teacher use to perform her speech and/or that of others? What does this tone indicate about how the teacher feels about herself and others? |

stances that are coming together. Teachers' narratives, then, are sites where multiple contexts intersect and overlap, enabling teachers to orient to these multiple and overlapping interactional contexts relationally—a process described henceforth as "intercontextuality" (Floriani, 1994)—to present themselves in a certain light.

Wortham (2001) has named such a focus on the interactional layer of stories a *dialogic narrative analysis*. Dialogism can offer teacher educators a tool for prompting teachers to reconsider their past selves and viewpoints in light of their present circumstances. When analyzing a teacher's story for interaction, teacher educators focus analytically on the relationships between contexts and between the teacher and her audience (see Table 4.4).

TABLE 4.4.
Questions Pursued in a Dialogic Analysis of Teachers' Narratives

| AREAS OF INQUIRY | QUESTIONS |
| --- | --- |
| *Interactional contexts* | How does the storytelling context shape the teacher's narrative? |
| *Interactional history* | How is the teacher's narrative shaped by her interactions with the teacher educator and/or other listeners? |
| *The narrated context* | What contexts can be identified in the teacher's narrative? What is the context of the events she reports? How does the narrated context interact with the storytelling context as a meaning-making device? |

Examining the content and structure of a story presents a model for uncovering one's viewpoints, whereas teachers' viewpoints unfold through their interactions with teacher educators, classroom teachers, classmates, and others.

## A LAYERED INTERPRETATION
## OF LINDSEY MAXWELL'S STORY

To understand what these layers of interpretation can allow teacher educators to see and hear in teacher's stories, I return to Lindsey's story. After analyzing Lindsey's story for each of these layers, I then propose some practical implications of such analysis for teacher educators.

### Analyzing Theme

In "You Had to Convince Your Parents," Lindsey Maxwell discusses how she struggled with her parents, particularly her father, over acquiring at-home technology access. She recounts how she and her brother helped her father recognize the educational value of technology. Once this feat was accomplished, her father was willing to have Internet access at home. Throughout the course of her narration, the following themes emerge: (1) struggling with parents (i.e., authority figures) over literacy materials, and (2) convincing parents (i.e., authority figures) to allow technology use.

These themes were similar to those that emerged in other preservice teachers' stories. For instance, another teacher who participated in this study, Rachel Rosenberg, recounted the following story, which describes a conflict that she had with her high school yearbook teacher:

> We had like a really old guy who was our yearbook person and he was like, "I've been doing this since 1963. And I know they have those computer programs to do it now but I think they're silly." Which really sucked because we had to take this computer class, so we all knew desktop publishing, like we'd learned it. We were like: "There's such a better way to do this." And he was like, "No. Rubber cement, end those pages, and cut it out, and. . . ."

These themes of struggling with and convincing authority figures to use technology reveal an important facet of these teachers' identities—that is, they are agents in their literacy learning. Lindsey and Rachel describe how they successfully convinced male authority figures to bring newer forms of technology and material resources into their literacy practices. In analyzing for this theme, then, we come to understand how Lindsey is like or unlike other Euro-American, female teachers in her literacy learning.

## Analyzing Form

If we categorize Lindsey's story into its narrative components, we see how she uses certain aspects of structure to convey meaning (see Table 4.5).

TABLE 4.5.
Narrative Form of "You Had to Convince Your Parents"

| TEACHER EDUCATOR'S FRAMING QUESTION | AMY: *Did you surf it [the Internet] at home too? Did you have it at home?* |
|---|---|
| Abstract | Lindsey: That was—I remember that was a big deal trying to get the Internet at home *[A: yeah]*. |
| Orientation | Like it was—like it was—like you had to convince your parents that it was necessary to have this—this tool at home. It was like, "Do you understand the capabilities? Like either you spend, ya know, how many hundreds of dollars on like an encyclopedia set." *[A: right]* And th- that's what we were debating whether we should get an encyclopedia set or the Internet. And I remember having these conversations with my parents and I'm like, "Its constantly updated." My dad still doesn't regularly use the Internet. He doesn't like using it. *[A: uh huh]* He's just not—he doesn't understand it. Like *[A: uh huh]* |
| Complications | I remember at one point we got it hooked up where we had some telephone—it was like a telephone system or something *[A: yeah, yes]* on the computer and you could call people in different countries. And we called somebody in South Africa. And my dad thought it was just the strangest thing in the world that you could talk to someone in South Africa from [Messina]. *[A: hhh]* |
| | And we were like: "What—what is going on here, ya know?" *[A: uh huh]* |
| Resolution | And he was having all these conversations *[A: laughing]* and I think it was at that point that he was finally sold (.) *[A: uh huh]* on the idea of having a computer and having, ya know, *[A: uh huh]* all of these resources that, "Hey. This—this could be a really cool thing and a good learning opportunity for my kids." *[A: uh huh]* |
| Evaluation | But trying to get it was just— |

Lindsey invests the bulk of her narrative efforts in setting the scene of her story, situating her story within overlapping settings, which together compel her response. First, Lindsey sets her story within the social milieu of the mid-1990s, where youth such as Lindsey "had to convince [their] parents that it was necessary to have this tool at home." This general milieu was one where youth struggled with their parents over getting the Internet at home rather than having an encyclopedia set. Having established the general climate, Lindsey situates her story within a more local setting, illustrating how this general climate emerges within the particularities of her home life: "And that's what we were debating, whether we should get an encyclopedia set or the Internet. And I remember having these conversations with my parents."

Finally, Lindsey connects past and present settings, locating her story within a more present-tense local setting, one where her father "still doesn't regularly use the Internet." This final layer of setting contextualizes the problematic experience that she is about to narrate as existing not just within the relationships of parents and their children or within the relationship of Lindsey's parents and Lindsey, but also within the disposition and character of Lindsey's father himself: "He doesn't like using it. He's just not—he doesn't understand it."

Setting her story in this way allows Lindsey to explore her own identity and how she is like others within her peer group. As a teacher educator, this kind of insight into Lindsey's story tells me that Lindsey sees herself and her life experiences as being typical for an individual her age, and that she is speaking as a representative of her peer group. As such, Lindsey does not indicate that she is aware that some youth have not had the same access to these high-technology literacy materials as she has.

## Analyzing Language and Grammar

In telling her story, Lindsey uses language and grammar to get her point across. One feature that stands out is how she portrays speech. Verbs such as "convince" and "debate" depict the interactions between herself and her parents and highlight her agency: "You had to <u>convince</u> your parents" and "That's what we were <u>debating</u>." Lindsey chooses to frame these interactions using this language of conflict.

In the setting component, we might also consider how she uses the progressive aspect to emphasize the iterative nature of her debates with her parents: "That's what we <u>were debating</u>, whether we should get an encyclopedia set or the Internet" and "I remember <u>having these conversations</u> with my parents." In the latter of these two related excerpts, Lindsey emphasizes the repeated quality of these conversations, using "remember" in place of the "be" component of the progressive (see e.g.,

Rymes, 2001, p. 45). We could hypothesize that the deployment of the progressive aspect enables Lindsey to play up the ongoing nature of the contexts in which these experiences are rooted.

Another notable storytelling technique that Lindsey employs to deepen the hue of her narrative is revoicing the words of other characters and herself. We might analyze how this revoiced speech or "constructed dialogue" (Tannen, 1989) works differently in the different narrative components. For instance, in setting the scene of her narrative, Lindsey uses constructed dialogue to create a general depiction of her activity in getting the Internet at home, revoicing: "It's constantly updated." This subtle instance of constructed dialogue could be construed as highlighting Lindsey's participation in the debates with her parents and conveying a general sense of Lindsey's agency in this endeavor.

In her response component, however, Lindsey uses constructed dialogue as a technique for characterizing her father. The sentence, "Hey! This could be a really cool thing and a good learning opportunity for my kids," could be approached as framing her father's change of mind in a particular way, suggesting his sense of surprise at the Internet's capabilities. We might look at this textual recasting, then, as enabling Lindsey to suggest a new identity for her father, that of a "good parent" who is willing to procure learning resources for his children. This recasting of her father's identity emerges in light of her perspectives on what constitutes a good parent as well as her agency in procuring technological resources for herself.

These examples of how Lindsey uses constructed dialogue to recast the speech of herself and others in her narrative do not, in and of themselves, convey Lindsey's perspectives on these past events. But their repeated occurrence in this narrative, along with other structural choices that Lindsey makes, deepens and complicates who Lindsey and her antagonists are and what they believe and value.

## Analyzing for Interaction

If we consider how "You Had to Convince Your Parents" unfolded through an interaction between Lindsey and her audience (me, the teacher educator), then we can gain insight into the coauthoring of teachers' narratives, how someone telling a story is closely influenced by how their listeners respond. Through stories, aspiring teachers and teacher educators can build shared ways of understanding their experiences, their teaching, their pedagogies, and their students' learning. Telling stories with teacher educators may enable preservice teachers to develop and enact certain identities or to reframe their stories and the perspectives that are enacted within them.

Wortham's dialogic analysis allows us to understand that the way a teacher tells a story is closely influenced by how teacher educators (or other listeners) respond. Through stories, teachers and teacher educators can build shared ways of understanding their experiences, their teaching, their pedagogies, and their students' learning. Telling stories with teacher educators may enable teachers to develop and enact certain identities and reframe their stories and, thus, reframe their viewpoints. By understanding how teachers are positioning themselves and others in their stories, teacher educators can better support teachers in analyzing and reframing those stories. In Lindsey's story, dialogic analysis asks us to consider how the interactional context and Lindsey's prior relationship with the teacher educator (me) impact the kinds of identities she enacts and the viewpoints she invokes.

For teacher educators, the overarching context in which teachers' narratives emerge holds particular consequences for co-authorship. For instance, "You Had to Convince Your Parents" was generated during a research interview with Lindsey. Because this was a life history interview, Lindsey was told that the purpose was for her to talk as much as she felt like about various aspects of her life. Telling a story in response to an interview question was not an entirely unique occurrence; in fact, I aimed to create a context that would support Lindsey's storytelling.

Co-authoring allows us to understand that storytelling is not a neutral activity. In telling stories, teachers emphasize certain events or omit details depending on their listener. In teacher education contexts, teachers usually tell stories to a group of other teachers or to an experienced teacher educator. These interactional relationships shape what teachers choose to say and the kinds of language they use for portraying the narrated events. At various moments in Lindsey's storytelling, she drew on her relationship with the teacher educator to communicate meaning, at times positioning herself as a student and me as a teacher educator. This teacher educator-student positioning left different impressions depending on who initiated it. The teacher educator references her role as a teacher to clarify any prior information that Lindsey has conveyed about her life. Lindsey references herself as a student when she is trying to "teach" the teacher educator about the social conditions of schooling experienced by herself and her peers. In short, Lindsey enacts the role of "knowledge-haver" with teachers, her father, and her classmates. Largely, this enactment leaves the impression that Lindsey exerts authority and power in her interactions with the teacher educator and other individuals like her who have played the authority role within her life. The interactional context, then, can be generally characterized as a forum where Lindsey exerts authority. Understanding the storytelling context in this way makes other information salient that is conveyed throughout the course of Lindsey's storytelling.

The talk preceding this narrative is important to consider for understanding co-authoring. Lindsey talked at length about the technology resources to which she had access in her high school. Somewhat unabashedly, she describes her high school as being sated with technological resources:

> We had a brand-new building. It was like 2 years old when I got there. And we had this beautiful library, and it was like the center of the building. It's gorgeous. And there's like skylights in the library. And the librarians bring you in. And they teach you how to use like all these different machines. And at that time there were still card catalogs, but they were starting to go to more of an online system where you could type in any book or author and find it. We had a couple computer labs.

> There was an old computer lab that was mostly for juniors and seniors because that was in their wing. But there were computers in the library. There was a station of six that we could use. And then there was also a separate computer lab off the library that there was enough to seat the whole class in there.

In response to this description of the materials available to her in school, Lindsey is asked to describe how this is related to the resources made available at her home. As we can see, the questions, "Did you surf it at home? Did you have it at home too?" do not explicitly trigger Lindsey's storytelling. However, these questions do make certain aspects of the context salient and do offer Lindsey certain resources for providing an elaborated narrative response. For example, the questions in "You Had to Convince Your Parents" signal a structural shift from the context indexed in the preceding talk (Lindsey's high school). In this way, the questions presuppose the context of the narrated events. Indeed, following these questions, Lindsey shifts from talk about the Internet at her high school to talk about the Internet at her home.

Looking closely at the unfolding of Lindsey's story is just one way to understand the co-authoring of teachers' narratives. Positioning offers another means for understanding co-authoring. As teachers and teacher educators engage in storytelling, they each bring to the interaction their specific histories, they presuppose the histories of their fellow interactants, and they presume a history for any of the other individuals who become characters in their telling. Each social position carries with it particular viewpoints about what is appropriate and acceptable behavior toward oneself and others. In enacting and creating social positions for themselves and others, storytelling enables teachers to bring different social positions into interaction with one another.

In "You Had to Convince Your Parents," Lindsey creates the voices of six different characters: Lindsey as "all" youth, Lindsey in high school, "all" parents, Lindsey's parents, Lindsey's family, and Lindsey's father. "All" parents and Lindsey's parents, in particular, do not speak with a voice that plays any distinctive role in this story. But the four other characters do speak with identifiable voices that recur throughout this story. Through these characters' voices, Lindsey presents herself as a youth who is entitled to certain technology resources, and she presents her parents as being obligated to invest in these technology resources for her schooling. Specifically, she presents this story as if she is speaking for all youth: "You had to convince your parents." She also dramatizes what we can take to be a recurring experience for youth like Lindsey, having to plead with their parents to invest in this technology: "It was like/do you understand the capabilities/like either you spend ya know/ how many hundreds of dollars on like an encyclopedia set." Lindsey characterizes her parents, particularly her father, as being "behind the times" and technologically naïve, supplying a motive for his reluctance to invest in the Internet: "My dad still doesn't regularly use the Internet/ he doesn't like using it/ which is not—he doesn't understand it." Lindsey presents herself as more technologically capable, experienced, and savvy than her father. Yet her father is the sort of parent who, when the utility of a resource for his children's education is made clear, will willingly procure and invest in that resource. Lindsey holds her father accountable, however, for his unwillingness to invest initially in the Internet, suggesting that "getting" the Internet should not have been such a struggle: "But trying to get it was just." Through her description of this event to the interviewer, Lindsey positions herself interactionally within events being narrated. We see Lindsey, for instance, portraying herself as several different kinds of characters: "all" youth, a child, a technology savvy individual. This positioning of herself is mostly accomplished by up-playing her father's technological naïveté: "My dad still doesn't regularly use the Internet . . . he doesn't understand it." Through these self-portrayals, Lindsey foregrounds her agency, technology knowledge, and sense of entitlement to technology resources.

Lindsey enacts these characters for me as a teacher educator, a relationship mediated by the present context in which she has just completed a literacy methods course that focused extensively on using new literacies and technologies as part of the elementary literacy curriculum. Given this background information, Lindsey's portrayal of her father as a technology user can be understood as an appeal to my sensibilities as a teacher educator. Lindsey could be interpreted as saying: "Can you believe this? He still doesn't use the Internet. What kind of person doesn't use the Internet in this day and age?" She could reasonably expect me to agree given my known stance in class regarding these issues.

Looking closely at how the teacher educator gets involved in the narration of this story further reveals the co-authored nature of this evaluation of her father's technology. For instance, we can see the teacher educator participating in the narration with Lindsey, sharing her own personal experiences with at-home Internet use:

> L: I remember at one point we got it hooked up, where we had some telephone—it was a telephone system or something [TE: Yes] on the computer. And you could call people in different countries. [TE: Yes!] And we called somebody—[TE: My parents had that].

The interaction between Lindsey and the teacher educator suggests that this exchange is not solely between a teacher educator and a teacher but also between two individuals who are daughters and who have experienced similar interactions with their parents over new technologies.

According to the predominant explanation of a teacher's narratives, this representation of herself in these different ways might somehow lead Lindsey to reconsider the kinds of social privileges that she has experienced, which enabled her to see technology as a resource to which she was entitled. In her talk that follows "You Had to Convince Your Parents," Lindsey enacts new positions for herself, her father, and the teacher educator, presupposing the present context of her teacher education program in which she is encouraged to scrutinize her own social privileges.

> But trying to get it was just—[TE: Did you and your brother have to convince him?] Yeah, yeah it was the two of us and it—he was like, ya know, "What do you need it for? Why-why are you using this at school? And, what—what is this—what is this doing?" And, it's like well, ya know, all the research projects we have to do and all this other stuff. And then the whole, ya know, like email. And, it wasn't as much as—I don't—it's interesting, because now it seems like there's such an expectation that ALL students have email. And, that all students have this access to computers. And, like here [her apartment]. I don't have a phone. And, I don't have access to the Internet. So. [TE: Oh, no.] That's what I'm saying. Like and everybody—I mean, it's like an expectation that if you're at the University that you HAVE to have email. You HAVE to be able to communicate this way. But it's like, I don't. And the same with Hazel [a classmate], too. She doesn't have these regular things. She doesn't have—like, she's lucky if she gets to her computer once a week. But I mean like for people who can't afford it. I mean, I can afford my apartment, but I can't afford to have cable. I can't afford to have the Internet. So, it's like. . . .

At first glance, the previous characterization of herself may appear to be in opposition to the characterization established earlier, yet it is actually quite similar. Despite that Lindsey received the technology resources she needed for "doing" high school, we can see that Lindsey continues to cast herself as being deprived of the resources she needs. As she says, "You have to be able to communicate this way. But it's like, I don't." Here, we witness Lindsey acknowledging that technology is a resource required for school. However, as she points out, this resource requires a certain kind of economic capital that she currently does not have: "I mean like for people who can't afford it. I mean, I can afford my apartment, but I can't afford to have cable. I can't afford the Internet. I can't afford the extras."

This time, however, we are left with the impression that her father is not the "authority" who is doing the depriving. Rather, Lindsey casts the university as responsible for this deprivation because it reinforces expectations that all students must have access to computers as a requirement for the completion of their coursework: "I mean, it's an expectation that if you're at the university that you have to have email. You have to be able to communicate this way." The example of Hazel (Lindsey's former classmate and another of my former students) indicates that the teacher educator is also complicit. Such a change in Lindsey's position—from holding her father responsible to holding institutions responsible for the resources she needs to complete her education—is a significant moment in Lindsey's talk. In fact, this change in Lindsey's stance toward technology's necessity for schooling indicates that Lindsey recognizes the demands that institutions, such as schools, place on individuals—demands that can actually impact students' ability to complete the requirements for school: "Because now it seems like there's such an expectation that all students have email and that all students have this access to computers."

This kind of connection between her biography and the broader social and material conditions is what many teacher educators hope will happen when we use personal narratives in and beyond the classroom. Teacher educators want to see teachers zoom out from their immediate experiences, situate these experiences within broader social contexts, and shift the onus from the individual to the institution and society. Lindsey arrives at a place where she is able to critically reflect on her life experiences and how they have shaped her viewpoints on schooling.

## DISCUSSION: TAKING A MORAL STAND

Looking at the layers of Lindsey's story allows us to see how, through this story, Lindsey takes a moral stance (Ochs & Capps, 2001) toward the recounted events. As Ochs and Capps (2001) explain, a narrator's moral stance is "a disposition towards what is good or valuable and how one ought to live in the world" (p. 45). What makes "You Had to Convince Your Parents" a tellable story is how Lindsey sets her story within a context in which her parents violated her expectation of what is morally "good" parenting. That is, morally "good" parents furnish their children with the material resources necessary for schooling. From a moral perspective, then, Lindsey acted for the "good" (i.e., in pursuing high-technology literacies).

In reframing this story through her subsequent talk, Lindsey comes to reframe this moral stance. Taking the "higher moral ground," Lindsey frames institutions as violating her moral expectations. Recounting this story allows Lindsey to get at a bigger moral issue—that is, the roles that institutions can play in reproducing social inequities. Because literacy is always linked to access to material goods, interpreting the layers of a teacher's stories about literacy can help teacher educators better understand the moral perspectives that undergird teachers' practices.

So, Lindsey articulated moral viewpoints in her story. But how can such a layered interpretation be pedagogically useful for teacher educators? The moral aspects of narrative discourse are beginning to be explored in teacher educators' use of narratives (Johnson, 2008). In the next section, I use Lindsey's story to propose questions for reflection.

## Implications for Teacher Education: Prompting Reflection

The setting of "You Had to Convince Your Parents" is vital for understanding Lindsey's moral stance. In listening to teachers' stories, then, teacher educators can consider how the story setting is elaborated. Recall that Lindsey's story conveys the impression that Lindsey's experiences are typical for all youth of her peer group. Yet Lindsey says nothing about the access to economic resources that is needed to secure such technology resources at home. To call attention to such an absence in her narrative, it is useful to discuss the social context and the role of social class in the procurement of literacy resources. Lindsey could be asked:

> Set your story within another context. How does this new setting impact the way you tell your story?

Lindsey's selection of her setting enables her to morally evaluate methods for promoting literacy, persuading the listener that her father's behavior was somehow inappropriate and violated her expectations of how a parent should behave. As we aim to prepare teachers who value the equitable teaching of all children, we must listen carefully to the moral viewpoints that unfold in the stories they tell. In Lindsey's case, she could be asked:

> *Reflect on the events in your story. What do they suggest about what is "good" for parents to do in supporting their children's literacy learning? What factors might inhibit parents from acting in this way?*

A focus on narrative form alone is insufficient for triggering an aspiring teacher's critical engagement with her moral stance. Grammar and language play a key role in how a preservice teacher such as Lindsey portrays herself and construes her moral stance through narrative form. As a teacher educator, I find the linguistic and grammatical aspects of narrative tellings to be most compelling and salient for encouraging critical reflection on one's moral stance. Because it is through language that individuals represent and structure the events of their lives (cf. Capps & Ochs, 1995). In telling stories, teachers use words, grammar, and narrative structure "to weave a tale in which events are linked temporally, causally, and emotionally and protagonists are depicted with a particular evaluative hue" (Ochs & Capps, 1995, p. 13). To prompt such engagement, Lindsey might be asked:

> *Think about how you represent the speech of others. What does such word choice or tone of voice reveal about your perceptions of those individuals and their actions? What other words or tone might you use to represent their speech?*
>
> *Think about your choice of verb tense. What does such verb tense reveal about how you think about these narrated events and your experience of them? Try changing the verb tense. How does this change in verb tense change the moral perspective of the story?*

Finally, stories are always told in contexts—near or distant. Such contexts shape what is said and how it is said. Teacher educators should encourage teachers to reflect on the role of context in narrative tellings. In Lindsey's case, she might be encouraged to reflect on her position as a student within an undergraduate teacher education program. She might be asked to consider how the views on literacy that circulate within this context influence her views on what is "good" and "right" in literacy teaching. Lindsey might be asked:

> *Consider what you have been learning about literacy in your teacher education program. What viewpoints on literacy do you see reflected in your story? How are these viewpoints consistent with those expressed in your teacher education program? How might these viewpoints be challenged or extended?*

The layered interpretations of Lindsey's story highlight the importance of narrative within teacher education. Through telling a story about an important moment in her literacy learning, Lindsey came to scrutinize the social privileges she experienced as a youth. As scholars coming from a sociocultural perspective on literacy have argued, what one defines as literacy, the purposes for which one uses literacy, and how one practices literacy are linked to an individual's cultural and social capital (Luke, 1994). Engaging preservice teachers in talk about how they learned literacy or other subject matters can offer teacher educators an avenue for exploring other aspects of their accumulated social privileges. In addition to asking preservice teachers to tell stories about their personal experiences, teacher educators could require them to tell stories about how they learned a certain subject matter, the materials they used for learning, and who "sponsored" (Brandt, 2001) them into that subject matter. Discussions about a concept as seemingly neutral as a subject matter area can provide a more comfortable and supportive entré into more charged discussions about race, class, and gender.

Likewise, part of urging teachers to engage critically with the biographical antecedents of their practices is encouraging them to consider their moral perspectives and how these give shape to their instructional choices. As I have shown, narrative analysis is one pedagogical tool for uncovering teachers' moral perspectives. However, getting at those moral precepts requires care in the form of careful listening and thoughtful analysis. In teacher education, our goal should be to care for the individuals we teach so that they might be able to "actualize" the "best" image they have for themselves (Noddings, 1986). Perhaps most important, this process of helping preservice teachers learn more about themselves as moral beings can offer them a model for doing this kind of work with their future students.

Questions for Reflection:

1. What are some of the contexts in which teachers and teacher candidates tell stories in your teacher preparation program (in courses, in the field, elsewhere)? How do you typically respond when teachers tell stories? How do teachers' peers and mentors typically respond to their stories?
2. Johnson suggests that a multilayered analysis (including thematic, formal, linguistic/grammatical, and dialogic analysis) can reveal teachers' moral viewpoints. Which type of analysis is most familiar to you? Which type of analysis would require you to stretch the most if you were to analyze teachers' stories? Why?
3. What is the value of probing teachers' stories with the questions that Johnson suggests in the concluding section of this chapter? Do you

foresee any possible pitfalls in posing such questions to teachers about their stories? Are there particular questions you think could be touchy for teachers with whom you work?

## REFERENCES

Brandt, D. (2001). *Literacy in American lives.* New York: Cambridge University Press.

Capps, L., & Ochs, E. (1995). *Constructing panic: The discourse of agoraphobia.* Boston: Harvard University Press.

Clandinin, D. J., & Connelly, F. M. (1986). Rhythms in teaching: The narrative study of teachers' personal practical knowledge of classrooms. *Teaching and Teacher Education, 2*(4), 377–387.

Clandinin, D. J., & Connelly, F. M. (1995). *Teachers' professional knowledge landscapes.* New York: Teachers College Press.

Clandinin, D. J., & Connelly, F. M. (2000). *Narrative inquiry: Experience and story in qualitative research.* San Francisco: Jossey-Bass.

Connelly, F. M., & Clandinin, D. J. (1988). *Teachers as curriculum planners: Narratives of experience.* New York: Teachers College Press.

Connelly, F. M., & Clandinin, D. J. (1990). Stories of experience and narrative inquiry. *Educational Researcher, 19*(5), 2–14.

Floriani, A. (1994). Negotiating what counts: Roles and relationships, texts and contexts, content and meaning. *Linguistics and Education, 5,* 241–274.

Florio-Ruane, S. (2001). *Teacher education and the cultural imagination: Autobiography, conversation, and narrative.* Mahwah, NJ: Lawrence Erlbaum Associates.

Gee, J. P. (1985). The narrativization of experience in the oral style. *Journal of Education, 167*(1), 9–34.

Gee, J. P. (1986). Units in the production of narrative discourse. *Discourse Processes, 9,* 391–422.

Gee, J. P. (1991). A linguistic approach to narrative. *Journal of Narrative and Life History, 1,* 15–39.

Gee, J. P. (1996). *Social linguistics and literacies: Ideology in discourses* (2nd ed.). Philadelphia, PA: Falmer Press.

Gomez, M. L. (1994). Teacher education reform and beginning teachers' perspectives on teaching "other people's" children. *Teaching and Teacher Education, 10*(3), 319–334.

Gomez, M. L., & Abt-Perkins, D. (1995). Sharing stories of teaching for practice, analysis, and critique. *Education Research and Perspectives, 22*(1), 39–52.

Gomez, M. L., & Tabachnick, B. R. (1992). Telling teaching stories. *Teacher Education, 4*(2), 129–138.

Gomez, M. L., Walker, A. B., & Page, M. L. (2000). Personal knowledge as a guide to teaching. *Teaching and Teacher Education, 16*(7), 731–747.

Heath, S. B. (1983). *Ways with words: Language, life, and work in communities and classrooms.* Cambridge, UK: Cambridge University Press.

Jefferson, G. (1978). Sequential aspects of storytelling in conversation. In J. Schenkein (Ed.), *Studies in the organization of conversational interaction* (pp. 219–248). New York: Academic Press.

Johnson, A. S. (2008). The moral of the story: Agency in preservice teachers' literacy stories. *English Education, 40*(2), 122–144.

Knobel, M. (1999). *Everyday literacies: Students, discourse, and social practice.* New York: Peter Lang.

Labov, W. (1972). *Language in the inner city: Studies in the Black vernacular.* Philadelphia: University of Pennsylvania Press.

Labov, W., & Waletsky, J. (1967/1997). Narrative analysis: Oral versions of personal experience. *Journal of Narrative and Life History, 7*(1–4), 3–38.

Lankshear, C. (1997). *Changing literacies.* Philadelphia: Open University Press.

Liston, D. P., & Zeichner, K. M. (1991). *Teacher education and the social conditions of schooling.* New York: Routledge.

Luke, A. (1994). Genres of power? Literacy education and the production of capital. In R. Hasan & G. Williams (Eds.), *Literacy in society.* London: Longman.

McVee, M. (2004). Narrative and the exploration of culture in teachers' discussions of literacy, identity, self, and other. *Teaching and Teacher Education, 20*(8), 881–899.

New London Group. (2000). A pedagogy of multiliteracies: Designing social futures. In B. Cope & M. Kalantzis (Eds.), *Multiliteracies: Literacy learning and the design of social futures* (pp. 9–37). New York: Routledge.

Noddings, N. (1986). Fidelity in teaching, teacher education, and research for teaching. *Harvard Educational Review, 56*(4), 496–510.

Ochs, E., & Capps, L. (2001). *Living narrative: Creating lives in everyday storytelling.* Cambridge, MA: Harvard University Press.

Rosenwald, G. C., & Ochberg, R. L. (Eds.). (1992). *Storied lives: The cultural politics of self-understanding.* New Haven, CT: Yale University Press.

Rymes, B. (2001). *Conversational borderlands: Language and identity in an alternative urban high school.* New York: Teachers College Press.

Schiffrin, D. (1994). *Approaches to discourse.* Oxford: Blackwell.

Street, B. V. (1984). *Literacy in theory and practice.* Cambridge, UK: Cambridge University Press.

Street, B. V. (1995). *Social literacies: Critical approaches to literacy in development, ethnography, and education.* London: Longman.

Tannen, D. (1989). *Talking voices: Repetition, dialogue, and imagery in conversational discourse.* Cambridge, UK: Cambridge University Press.

Titone, C. (1998). Educating the white teacher as ally. In J. L. Kincheloe, S. R. Steinberg, N. M. Rodriguez, & R. E. Chennault (Eds.), *White reign: Deploying whiteness in America* (pp. 159–175). New York: St. Martin's Press.

Wetherell, C., & Noddings, N. (Eds.). (1991). *Stories lives tell: Narrative and dialogue in education.* New York: Teachers College Press.

Wortham, S. (2001). *Narratives in action: A strategy for research and analysis.* New York: Teachers College Press.

# 5

## CLASSROOM NARRATIVES AND ETHICAL RESPONSIBILITY
### How Markers of Difference Can Inform Teaching and Teacher Education

*Stephanie L. Kerschbaum*

One of the more intimidating elements of designing a course or curriculum, particularly for new teachers, is the sheer unpredictability of the classroom environment. This unpredictability comes out of the fact that classrooms bring together diverse individuals who must learn to work together to achieve educational goals. To help the classroom become a productive learning environment for all students, one of the most important tasks for teachers is to learn about the others with whom they are sharing classroom spaces. Gleaning knowledge about who students are can make the difference between creating a classroom environment that supports their learning versus one that frustrates students' motivations for learning.

There are many sources of information that teachers can draw on to help them learn about their students and how best to design their classrooms. One source that has been fruitfully explored in teacher-education research is students' home environments and communities. For example, through ethnographic research into out-of-school lives and communities, literacy researchers Shirley Brice Heath (1983) and Victoria Purcell-Gates (1997) showed just how powerful knowledge about home literacy practices could be for helping teachers make their lessons more accessible to diverse students. Purcell-Gates' and Heath's research led to an explosion of research focusing on understanding the complex relationships between "school culture" and other communities (see e.g., Hull & Schultz, 2002). Taking into account the richness of this area of scholarship, this chapter focuses on understanding how, within the classroom, teachers can make sense of the complex array of experiences, behaviors, and ways of being in the world that are emerging. A key question that I ask is: How can teachers learn to observe their own classrooms and attend to what they and their students are doing? How, in Schultz's (2003) terms, can teachers "listen" to their classrooms?

Many teachers are already highly reflective about their teaching as they spend time thinking about past actions and how they might learn from what they have experienced (e.g., Dyson, 2003). In this chapter, I suggest that narrative analysis is a powerful resource for teachers who are interested in improving the way they take advantage of the information that students display about themselves within the classroom. Although much of what teachers and students do and say in the classroom is deeply informed by experiences that happen outside of it—at home, among friends, around the community—they are still fostering new relationships, identities, and ways of being in the world (Gee, 1996) within the classroom. Thus, this chapter, taking as a focus the problem of negotiating and engaging differences, suggests that a closer look at classroom narratives and the relationships that these narratives reveal has much to convey to teachers seeking to both learn *about* and *with* their students. However, as I discuss in more detail later, it is important to remember that the narrative analyses I display would be enriched with additional contextual and environmental information about these students and their lives. Thus, narrative analysis acts as a complement to other approaches for learning about and engaging with students.

## WHAT IS NARRATIVE ANALYSIS?

Telling narratives is one way that individuals compose life worlds for themselves and others. Through narratives, people evoke many different contexts, settings, and environments, and narrative tellers frequently populate their stories with characters who perform actions in the narrative world. The power of narrative for shaping worldviews (see Holland et al., 1998) and constructing identities (e.g., Wilkerson, 2000) is one reason that it has been a particularly fruitful research site within schools of education. As a method for uncovering the relationships and positions that individuals take with regard to one another, sociolinguistic narrative analysis looks at the resources—linguistic and otherwise—that are used by speakers as they share stories. Sociolinguistic narrative analysts also take into consideration the social contexts in which stories are told and how they are responded to and shaped by other participants in an interaction.

I argue here that looking at the ways that lives are constructed in classroom narratives alongside the linguistic resources drawn on to do so can help teachers and teacher educators as they learn *with* and *from* others within their classrooms. To show more concretely how this work happens, I perform a brief analysis of three student narratives using the following guiding questions:

- How does an examination of narrative telling shed light on engagement with difference?
- What ethical responsibilities are revealed through this examination?
- What implications do these questions offer for teacher education?

In responding to these questions, I suggest how sociolinguistic narrative analysis sheds light on how individuals learn about one another over the course of everyday interaction. In addition, these analyses suggest directions for considering the ethical responsibilities teachers and students have with regard to one another. As classrooms continue to diversify in myriad ways, it becomes more and more important for teachers to develop resources that they can use to learn from (and about) their students.

## PERSPECTIVES FOR INTERPRETING NARRATIVES

At this point, I want to introduce an orientation to difference and an ethical framework that I have developed for this analysis, built on the work of Mikhail Bakhtin (1981, 1990, 1993). My approach to difference takes as a foundation the importance of maintaining an open stance with regard to others. An open stance is important because not all differences are readily recognizable, and even those differences that may seem apparent at first sight may not be those that are most relevant in a particular interaction. Learning how to make use of the knowledge generated through narrative and narrative analysis necessitates understanding differences as myriad, dynamic, and negotiated. In addition, we must hold ourselves responsible for learning about, and with, others—learning about others is not a passive activity, but a highly interactive one.

### What Is Difference?

To illustrate the complexity of difference, let me first offer an example. Consider how talk about categories of race and gender within teacher education do not fully constitute difference. Difference, rather than being a static property held by an individual, is negotiated among participants in an interaction. At any given moment, there are many differences that may be (or are becoming) salient for those involved. Thus, an important question to keep in mind is, "What differences are people negotiating between one another, and how are they relevant to the interaction at hand?"

When I describe myself as a white woman to my readers, I offer my racial identification as well as my gender as a source of information about me. However, my whiteness and my femaleness are not static components of my identity. Rather, I construct (or perform) whiteness and femaleness in different ways as I interact with different people. Those aspects of my identity become more and less relevant in different interactions, and I cannot assume beforehand the significance that those pieces of information will play in an interaction—relevance is co-constructed between participants in an interaction.[1] I am not suggesting that my whiteness or my femaleness *change* or that I am ever *not* white or *not* female. Rather, what I am saying is that my race and gender do not have the *same* meaning in every interaction. I call on my race and gender (as well as other features of my identity) in different ways depending on who I am interacting with and where those interactions are taking place.

The dynamism of these features of my identity—whiteness, femaleness—comes, in part, because differences are always relational. Because no two people can occupy the same physical or conceptual spaces, all encounters with others are *always* encounters with difference. In addition, because no two people are standing with the same perspective, it is impossible for either of them to fully know or, in Bakhtin's (1990) terms, "consummate" the other.[2] The noncoincidence of individual selves highlights the fact that, for there to be difference, there must be more than one person involved. Nobody is, in and of themselves, inherently "different." People are always different *from* someone or something else. It is by identifying a difference between one self and another that people come to know who they are. As Bakhtin's work shows, people cannot know themselves until they can learn ways that they are, and can be, named, defined, or otherwise positioned. I am only white, for instance, in relation to other people with different racial and ethnic identifications; I am only female in relation to people with different gender identifications. Understanding that I can be positioned as white and female comes only through encounters with those who show me that those categories have some kind of meaning—that is, through encounters with difference.

The situatedness of difference emphasizes that differences are negotiated: The differences that I may perceive between myself and my interlocutors are not necessarily the same differences that they may be identifying. In this sense, differences are negotiated; they are not simply "out there" waiting to be named or plucked out of thin air. Negotiations of difference are challenging precisely because they require that we do more than simply identify and name differences; we must also work to understand what those differences might mean and how they position people with regard to one another. Power and authority, for example, are not permanent states that individuals occupy in relation to others; rather, they are products of interactional efforts and situational conditions. These features of difference lend themselves to an analytic approach that facilitates close attention to the work taking place during mundane interactions to make sense of how difference is used by participants in the course of such activity.

## An Ethical Responsibility: Answerable Engagement

Underlying this orientation to difference is a model of interpersonal interaction that I call "answerable engagement." This theory is derived from Bakhtin's (1990, 1993) early philosophical writings, as well as research in composition studies and education that has begun to move beyond a focus on dialogism to incorporate Bakhtin's ethical theories (e.g., Bialostosky, 1999; Halasek, 1999; Hicks, 1996, 2000; Juzwik, 2004). Although dialogism is concerned with what folklorist Richard Bauman (2004) describes as "the orientation of the now-said to the already-said and the to-be-said" (p. 5), answerable engagement incorporates what Juzwik (2004) has called the morally weighty moment of being in everyday interaction. Answerability places responsibility on individuals to respond to others and to hold themselves accountable for those utterances. In all interactions, differences emerge that affect the direction of future talk and interaction. Because of the consequences that our language and talk can have on others, it's imperative for us to direct our activity toward others in ethically responsible ways.

This framework provides a foundation for the sociolinguistic narrative analysis in this chapter because it takes seriously the identity work that students and teachers do with one another in the classroom. How do students articulate their awareness of difference in their interactional positioning and responses to the others with whom they are sharing classroom space? How are these differences openly acknowledged? Before I move into the narrative analysis, I talk briefly about the study in which I collected these narratives.

## THE LARGER STUDY: CONTEXT AND BACKGROUND

The following narratives came from a larger project focusing on how students learn to communicate with one another across differences. Situated in a university writing classroom, the study looked at the role that literacy—specifically, writing—played in promoting students' engagement with difference. At the time I collected the data, the school, a large, majority-white state university, was midway through a 10-year diversity agenda focused on recruiting and retaining specific ethnic populations at the school. The classroom I studied was also part of the university's First Year Experience Program, in which a group of 20 students took three classes together and lived near one another on campus.

Data generated during this study included field notes from participant observations, audiotapes and transcripts of all class sessions over the course of the semester, video and audiotapes of selected small-group peer review groups, interviews with focal students and the course instructor, and copies of students' essay portfolios as well as all textual materials distributed in class. In addition, I gathered documents related to the Composition Program, the First Year Experience Program, and the university's diversity initiatives. (For a more detailed description of the study design and context, see Kerschbaum [2005].) Narratives were identified from transcripts of students' talk during class. In the next section, I explain how narratives were identified and provide an entry into narrative study. I then move into an analysis of three student narratives taken from this body of data.

## IDENTIFYING AND ANALYZING NARRATIVES

An important issue within narrative analysis is that of what "counts" as a narrative. According to sociologist William Labov (1972; Labov & Waletzky, 1997), a minimal narrative is one that contains at least one temporal juncture. A temporal juncture is a string of at least two clauses that are linked by a causal or sequential order—that is, events that are told in the same order in which they actually occurred. However, many narratives, as Ochs and Capps (2001) point out, do not relate past events in a linear, chronological sequence. Some narratives, for instance, may foreshadow future events or jump around sequentially. To broaden the definition of narrative to include such accounts, Ochs and Capps suggest understanding temporality as one of five narrative dimensions. They articulate a continuum of narrative time, moving from narratives that are told in a linear fashion toward narratives that have diverse, uncertain paths. Events may be rearranged or displayed in a different order than they occurred, they may be projected into the future, or they may even be cast hypothetically. As Ochs and Capps write, "temporal elasticity lies at the very heart of personal narrative, in that narrative time is human time, and human time flows back and forth from moments remembered, to the unfolding present, to moments imagined" (p. 200).

Following this definition of the temporality of narrative, stretches of conversation where students described a series of actions, events, or moments for their peers were pulled out from the class transcripts. After this collection of student narratives was generated, the stories were sorted into three broad topic-based categories. These categories—literacy reenactments, extra-academic experiences, and other school-based experiences—helped show when, and for what purposes, students told stories. The number of narratives told in each category fluctuated over the course of the semester depending on a variety of factors, such as the familiarity of the students in a group with one another, surrounding events (e.g., Halloween weekend or Thanksgiving break), interpersonal dynamics of particular groups (groups changed with each peer review session), as well as where students were in the revision process.

Categorizing students' narratives, while providing important information about the function of narratives in the classroom, did not reveal much about *how* the students were telling stories. To understand the ways that narratives were being told, it was important to break the narratives down into smaller units that would enable close examination of other elements of the talk. In this analysis, narratives are divided into lines and stanzas. Each line represents what is uttered in between one breath or between pauses. Each stanza is a cluster of lines focusing around one main function. As Gee (1996) writes, each stanza provides *one* perspective, "such that when character, place, time, event, or the function of a piece of information changes . . . the stanza must change" (pp. 94–95). Breaking the narratives up in this way helps show relationships among various elements of the narratives, such as topic orientations and shifts in tone, speaker, subject positions, or verb tenses. The importance of stanzas in making sense of the ways that students position themselves through narrative will become clearer below when I walk through a stanza-by-stanza comparison of two student narratives. More detailed transcription conventions are shown in Table 5.1.

## TABLE 5.1.
### Transcription Conventions

| | |
|---|---|
| Line breaks | what is uttered in between breaths or between pauses |
| Stanza breaks | each stanza is a cluster of lines focusing around one main function |
| : | Colon indicates elongated vowel sound; use of multiple colons indicates greater elongation (e.g., no:::w) |
| wow | Underlining indicates emphasis on word or part of word |
| [ | Two aligned brackets indicate overlapping talk is beginning |
| = | Latched discourse, continuous with previous or subsequent line |
| (she said) | Transcriber uncertainty or discourse inaudible |
| (*italics*) | Sounds or actions not captured in transcription |

## THREE STUDENT NARRATIVES

The three student narratives that form the heart of this analysis are displayed in Table 5.2. To help you understand what is happening at this point in the class conversation, I describe the classroom context and introduce the three women taking part in this conversation. Lindsey, Choua, and Blia were working in a small group giving reactions to each others' first essays. The students had written responses to one another's drafts before meeting in class, and much of their classroom conversation focused on reading aloud and elaborating their written feedback. As the three narratives are told, Blia and Choua have just finished communicating to Lindsey that she should not use the words "in conclusion" in her paper. To support this claim, Blia and Choua tell Lindsey that their previous teachers had instructed them not to write "in conclusion." In turn, Lindsey initiates a new topic—the beginning of the narrative sequence below—telling a story about her high school "college prep" class. Blia responds by relating a second narrative describing the rigor of her high school curriculum. In a third narrative, Lindsey solicits information from Blia about her high school and talks more about her own hometown. As you read, note the stanza divisions in the left-hand column.

TABLE 5.2.
A Narrative Engagement of Difference

| Stanza | | | Narrative 1: "We Never Like Wrote Papers in High School" |
|---|---|---|---|
| 1.1 | 1 | LINDSEY: | see we never like wrote papers in high school so |
| | 2 | BLIA: | oh wo:::w you are so::: lucky |
| | 3 | | [we had |
| | 4 | LINDSEY: | [no, we seriously wrote |
| | | | |
| 1.2 | 5 | | I had one like |
| | 6 | | my last |
| | 7 | ` | my senior year I had |
| | 8 | | uh college prep |
| | 9 | | like a college prep class= |
| | 10 | BLIA: | [mm-hmm |
| | | | |
| 1.3 | 11 | LINDSEY: | =[and we |
| | 12 | | the second semester |
| | 13 | | we wrote probably like two or three like |
| | 14 | | two page papers like |
| | 15 | | the first semester |

| 1.4 | 16 |          | and then the <u>whole</u> last semester |
|     | 17 |          | the <u>entire</u> last semester |
|     | 18 |          | was spent on writing a five page |
|     | 19 |          | double spaced paper |
|     | 20 | CHOUA:   | huh [the whole last semester |
|     | 21 | BLIA:    | [oh my |
|     | 22 | LINDSEY: | the whole last semester |
|     | 23 | CHOUA:   | I'm so (mad at) you guys |
| 1.5 | 24 | LINDSEY: | (*inaudible*) but anyway I was like |
|     | 25 |          | that was my college prep class |
|     | 26 | BLIA:    | [oh my god |
|     | 27 | LINDSEY: | [so |
|     | 28 | CHOUA:   | hhh |
|     | 29 | LINDSEY: | yeah |
|     | 30 | CHOUA:   | [it's so weird that |
|     | 31 | BLIA:    | [wow |
|     | 32 | CHOUA:   | [it's (???) |

*Stanza*   *Narrative 2: "We Had a Writing Across Curriculum Thing"*

| 2.1 | 33 | BLIA:    | [we went through <u>so</u> much trouble (too) |
|     | 34 |          | we had a writing across curriculum thing |
|     | 35 |          | where we had to write a paper for [every single class |
|     |    |          |                                          [(*hits table*) |
|     | 36 |          | [five paragraph theme |
|     |    |          | [(*hits table*) |
|     | 37 |          | (three of them) with the thesis and everything |
|     | 38 |          | every single semester |
|     | 39 |          | for all four years |
|     | 40 | LINDSEY: | [crappy |
| 2.2 | 41 | BLIA:    | [and they do (*laughs*) |
|     | 42 |          | they do uh |
|     | 43 |          | um |
|     | 44 |          | they keep track of how your writing |
|     | 45 |          | progresses over time |
| 2.3 | 46 |          | so |
|     | 47 |          | [that was like |
|     | 48 | LINDSEY: | [ohhhh <u>crappy</u> |
|     | 49 | BLIA:    | oh |
|     | 50 |          | it was awful |
| 2.4 | 51 |          | and then we had |
|     | 52 |          | our senior science project |

| | 53 | | which is like |
| | 54 | | um |
| | 55 | | a college |
| | 56 | | graduate research level sort of thing |
| | 57 | | yeah |
| 2.5 | 58 | | I had to do a |
| | 59 | | experiment |
| | 60 | | uh |
| | 61 | | find all the research that I like |
| | 62 | | you know |
| | 63 | | background information I need |
| | 64 | | analyze all the experiment data that I |
| | 65 | | got off my experiment |
| | 66 | | present it |
| | 67 | | in a |
| | 68 | | uh |
| | 69 | | like |
| | 70 | | uh |
| | 71 | | format |
| | 72 | | like |
| | 73 | | some people used overhead I used |
| | 74 | | Power Point and |
| 2.6 | 75 | | it was a competition |
| | 76 | | it was so hard (laughs) |
| | 77 | LINDSEY: | oh my God= |
| | 78 | BLIA | [so hard |
| | 79 | LINDSEY | =[we didn't do anything like that |

| Stanza | Narrative 3: "I Don't Know How I Ended Up Here" |

| 3.1 | 80 | LINDSEY: | I graduated from a class of 36 though |
| | 81 | BLIA: | oh I had |
| | 82 | | (well) mine was like 40 |
| | 83 | | 40 |
| | 84 | | something |
| 3.2 | 85 | LINDSEY: | yeah ours was like |
| | 86 | | what |
| | 87 | | was it private |
| | 88 | BLIA: | yeah |
| | 89 | | it's private |
| | 90 | LINDSEY: | okay ours was definitely public |
| | 91 | BLIA: | Oh |

| 3.3 | 92 | LINDSEY: | we had |
|---|---|---|---|
| | 93 | | like |
| | 94 | | kindergarten through 12 all in one building |
| | 95 | | like |
| | 96 | STUDENT: | (*laughing*) |
| | 97 | LINDSEY: | we were out in the boonies= |
| | 98 | BLIA: | [(*laughs*) |
| | 99 | LINDSEY: | =[never did anything |
| | 100 | | ever |
| | | | |
| 3.4 | 101 | | I don't know how I ended up here |
| | 102 | | no idea |
| | 103 | | but it's |
| | 104 | | it's worth it |
| | 105 | BLIA: | yeah |

## RESOURCES FOR ANALYZING NARRATIVES AND THE NEGOTIATION OF DIFFERENCE

Before we move into the analysis, I want to elaborate some resources that can be important for you in preparing to do analyses of this sort in classrooms. The first point to remember is that narratives should be treated dialogically (see also Johnson, Chapter 4, this volume; Rymes & Wortham, Chapter 3, this volume). Looking at narratives dialogically means that stories are not seen as simple vehicles of information about students. In Narrative 1, for instance, it is not enough to simply "learn" that Lindsey's college prep class did not assign much writing. For that to be the message of the narrative is to ignore the way that Lindsey's story is responding to Blia and Choua's earlier utterances, as well as how interpretations of her story change on hearing later utterances. When Lindsey talks further about her high school in Narrative 3, for instance, she does more than simply report features of her high school—she provides a narrative evaluation of that experience.

To understand how narratives evaluate, position, and reframe previous talk, it is important to analyze more than just what those narratives point to or reference. Dialogic analyses take into consideration relationships between the content of narratives and the linguistic and structural resources used to tell those stories. For instance, Wortham's (2000) analysis of an autobiographical narrative focuses on relationships between the storytelling event [the event of telling] and the narrated event [the events described in the story].[3] In a significant analysis of Jane's personal narrative, Wortham unpacks relationships between Jane-as-storyteller and Jane-as-character-in-her-story, calling attention to the linguistic resources that Jane drew on to position herself and her listener in particular ways.

For the purposes of the present analysis, we can use dialogic analyses of narrative not only to examine what differences are displayed and used when students tell narratives to each other but also to reveal how students are engaging those differences. Narrative, as a way of composing lives (Ochs & Capps, 2001), is also a way of *positioning* lives (Bamberg, 1997) and thus, of elaborating and giving meaning to difference. The fact that difference is everywhere speaks to the potential for any narrative telling to provide fodder for disagreement, conflict, disengagement, dissonance, resonance, alignment, identification, shared positioning, and support, among many other possibilities. These varied outcomes reinforce the importance of attending to the ways that our reactions to these narratives are both *responsive* and *responsible*. When we don't carefully consider how our talk may affect others (especially given the important role played by teachers' careful scaffolding of classroom talk (see e.g., Dyson, 1997a, 1997b, 2003), we may lose valuable opportunities for engaging students in the classroom conversation.

## But Just What Are We Responding/ Responsible To?

As speakers tell stories, and as they respond to others' stories, an important problem to consider is what speakers are picking up on as they construct their utterances. How do speakers live up to the responsibility they bear toward others? One way of examining such responsibility as exhibited through narrative is by identifying what I call "markers of difference." In developing this concept, I have borrowed—and somewhat transformed—the term "marker" from its sociolinguistic context, where the term "discourse marker" has been used to describe how speakers join together various elements of talk (Schiffrin, 1987). In the same sense that discourse markers act as "conversational glue" holding utterances together in some kind of relationship (Louwerse & Mitchell, 2003), markers of difference are used to articulate relationships between interlocutors—most specifically, relationships of identification and differentiation. Markers of difference function similarly to what Gumperz (1992) calls "contextualization cues," in the sense that they mediate speakers' and listeners' attention to the communicative event and the situation in which that communication is taking place.

In telling stories and relating information about themselves, people use markers to construct identities that are subsequently interpreted by those with whom they are interacting. In everyday talk, people use markers to describe themselves and respond to ways that they are situated by others. For instance, the following exchange shows Timothy responding to his perception of a "situated" *ethos* as he works to articulate the identity he wants to show his classmates:

| TIMOTHY: | only child single parent so me and mom are like super close it's insane like I'm not supposed to be friends with my mother |
| LUCY: | yeah you said you went shopping with your mom I was like man I can't go shopping with my mom |

Earlier in the conversation, Timothy talked about a failed shopping excursion where he and his mother had been trying to find attractive clothes for plus-sized women. In the previous quote, he offers up an explanation for the camaraderie he has with his mother. This explanation also suggests that Timothy thinks his peers may find his close relationship with his mother unusual, as he says, "It's insane like I'm not supposed to be friends with my mother." Lucy's reaction to Timothy's statement suggests that she picked up on that earlier discussion as a difference between herself and Timothy: "I was like man I can't go shopping with my mom." We see here Timothy purposefully displaying markers—"only child single parent"—as a way of constructing a self that indicates his awareness of social expectations as well as his own relationship to those expectations.

As an analytic resource, markers offer insight into *what* people are reacting to in one another's talk. As people choose (and sometimes don't choose) to display particular markers, they take up positions and identify themselves alongside others. Such positioning has much to do with markers that they have already read off one another's bodies and language, but it also has to do with the ever-changing meanings that are constructed in interaction. Markers are deeply dialogic because they are used by speakers at the same time that they are interpreted by others.

Although markers can be many different things—words, utterances, and objects (e.g., clothing, accessories)—the focus here is on how verbal markers are displayed within classroom narratives. But it's important to remember that there are many sources from which people draw information about others. Moreover, the verbal markers of difference that students and teachers engage in their talk are always interpreted in conjunction with other (visible and invisible) markers. As I discussed earlier, we often understand people as belonging to particular sociocultural categories based on the various sources of information we have about them.

One important source of information is precisely those markers that we perceive (e.g., of race, gender, disability, etc.) through interactions with others.

Now, let's analyze these three narratives with an eye toward understanding how Lindsey and Blia position themselves in sharing these stories, as well as how they display and respond to markers of difference in doing so.

## HOW IS DIFFERENCE OPERATING IN THESE NARRATIVES?

### Differential Positioning: A Stanza-by-Stanza Comparison

As we look at the three narratives displayed earlier, one thing to note early on is the way that Lindsey and Blia are explicitly positioning themselves alongside one another: Lindsey had one kind of high school experience (Narrative 1), and Blia had another kind of high school experience (Narrative 2). In these two narratives, various sociocultural differences are made explicit through the different positions the two women establish. As we turn to Narrative 3, ethical questions regarding how such positioning is functioning become important.

As she initiates the first narrative, Lindsey pronounces, "See we never like wrote papers in high school." What might Lindsey be responding to with this statement? One possibility is that she is identifying a difference between herself and her two peers. Unlike Blia and Choua, Lindsey did not write papers in high school. This may, in part, be a response to Blia and Choua's frequent references to their past writing instruction, as earlier in the conversation we hear Blia and Choua debating Modern Language Association (MLA) citation format, as well as mentioning what they had been taught about writing. As the narrative progresses, Lindsey provides evidence for how little writing she did during her college prep class (Lines 11–19).

In turn, when Blia launches into Narrative 2, she responds by recounting her own (different from Lindsey's) experience in high school. She tells of a rigorous academic culture, in which she produced a "senior science project" akin to a "college graduate research level sort of thing" (Lines 33–78). Note here that when Lindsey makes her first comment, "See we never wrote papers in high school" in line 1, Blia almost immediately begins to say "we had" (Line 3)—the same opening Blia later uses when she does tell Narrative 2, suggesting that her response may be, in part, motivated by Lindsey's *first* statement. A question to consider, then, is how what Blia has to say is influenced by both (a)

Lindsey's initial utterance, and (b) the details Lindsey relates in her narrative. Indeed, the two narratives are closely related. Structural similarities become especially apparent through a comparative stanza-by-stanza analysis. To facilitate the comparison, Narratives 1 and 2 are re-presented in Table 5.3 in a double-column format, and stanzas with parallel elements are juxtaposed.

Stanzas 1.1 and 2.1 both introduce the topic of each narrative: the two women's high school experiences with writing. We can usefully juxtapose Lindsey's experience with writing "in high school" in relation to Blia's more specific "writing across curriculum thing." Lindsey's description is more vague than Blia's; Blia recounts much more detail (as we see throughout Narrative 2) about her high school writing than Lindsey does. Both women frame their past experience using the first-person plural "we," showing that their writing experiences were not singular—they shared them with other students at their high schools. In addition to using the simple past tense, Blia and Lindsey are both describing past states or habitual actions: "We *never* like wrote" (Stanza 1.1, Line 1) and "We had to write a paper *for every single class*" (Stanza 2.1, Line 35). These ongoing activities set listeners up for a story that describes not an isolated experience but processes that were repeated (or not repeated, in Lindsey's case).

TABLE 5.3.
Different Experiences With High School Paper Writing

| Stza | Lindsey's Narrative (1) | | Blia's Narrative (2) | Stza |
|---|---|---|---|---|
| 1.1 | 1 LINDSEY: | see we never like wrote papers in high school so | 33 BLIA: [we went through <u>so</u> much trouble (too) | 2.1 |
| | 2 BLIA: | oh wo:::w you are <u>so:::</u> lucky | 34 we had a writing across curriculum thing | |
| | 3 | [we had | 35 where we had to write a paper for [every single class | |
| | 4 LINDSEY: | [no, we seriously wrote | [ (*hits table*) | |
| 1.2 | 5 | I had one like | 36 [five paragraph theme | |
| | 6 | my last | [(*hits table*) | |
| | 7 | my senior year I had | 37 (three of them) with the | |
| | 8 | uh college prep | thesis and everything | |
| | 9 | like a college prep class= | 38 every single semester | |
| | 10 BLIA: | [mm-hmm | 39 for all four years | |
| | | | 40 LINDSEY: [crappy | |

In Stanza 1.2, Lindsey moves from the more general situation that she describes in her first stanza to a more specific one as she bounds her account temporally to her final two semesters of high school: "My last/my senior year" (Lines 6–7), as well as to a particular course: "A college prep class" (Stanza 1.2, Line 9). We can understand this temporal bounding as one way for Lindsey to provide specific evidence for her claim in Stanza 1.1 that she "never like wrote papers in high school."

In Stanza 2.1, Blia does not restrict her account temporally. Instead, she chooses to elaborate general characteristics of the writing she did throughout high school: "Five paragraph theme / (three of them) with the thesis and everything." Blia discusses in some detail her experience throughout her high school years, whereas Lindsey focuses on her senior year early in her narrative. (It is not until Stanza 2.4 that Blia, in turn, focuses on her senior year.) One effect of this is that Blia is highlighting all the writing she did, whereas Lindsey spends more time elaborating the events of her college prep class.

Table 5.4 shows two stanzas in Blia's narrative that stand out because they contain elements that are not paralleled in Lindsey's first narrative.

Stanzas 2.2 and 2.3 of Blia's narrative incorporate two elements that are not found in Lindsey's narrative: a second character, "they" (Stanza 2.2), and an explicit evaluation of the narrative experience (Stanza 2.3). In Stanza 2.2, Blia describes how "*they* keep track of how your writing progresses over time" (Lines 44–45, italics added). She is probably referencing teachers or administrators who evaluated students' writing, so we

TABLE 5.4.
Different Evaluation of High School Paper Writing

| Stza | Lindsey's Narrative (1) | Blia's Narrative (2) | Stza |
|------|-------------------------|----------------------|------|
| | | 41  BLIA:   [and they do (*laughs*) | 2.2 |
| | | 42       they do uh | |
| | | 43       um | |
| | | 44       they keep track of how your writing | |
| | | 45       progresses over time | |
| | | 46       so | |
| | | 47           [that was like | 2.3 |
| | | 48  LINDSEY:  [ohhhh crappy | |
| | | 49  BLIA:   oh | |
| | | 50       it was awful | |

begin to see Blia positioning her narrative self alongside "they," who "kept track" of her progress in writing. In contrast, Lindsey does not reference any authority figure, teacher or otherwise, related to the "college prep" class she took. The characters created by the two women here suggest one difference in how they are constructing agency (the first level of positioning laid out by Bamberg [1997]). In these stanzas, Blia uses the present tense to describe what "they" do as a way to emphasize the duration of that activity over her 4 years in high school.

The second element, explicit evaluation of Blia's narrative, occurs in Stanza 2.3. Lindsey says, "[ohhhh crappy" (Line 48), to which Blia adds, "oh / it was awful." No parallel evaluation segment occurs during Lindsey's telling, save for Blia's "oh wo:::w you are so::: lucky" (Line 2) as Lindsey initiates her narrative. An important question to consider here is how Lindsey's interjected evaluation (note that her talk overlaps with Blia's in Lines 47 and 48) subsequently affects Blia's narrative telling. There are many possibilities here—Blia may have interpreted Lindsey's evaluation as evidence that Lindsey is impressed by how extensive Blia's writing experience was. Another possibility is that Lindsey's evaluation may have influenced Blia's own stance toward the amount of writing she did—as we see Blia reinforcing Lindsey's comment with "oh / it was awful." The two women are explicitly sharing values and attitudes toward writing in their co-evaluation of Blia's experience here. As we move into Stanzas 1.3 and 2.4 (see Table 5.5), we see both women moving toward specific moments of their high school writing experiences.

In Stanzas 1.3 and 2.4, Lindsey relates her "first-semester" writing experience, and Blia describes her "senior science project," which she likens to a "college / graduate research level sort of thing" (Stanza 2.4, Lines 52–56). The vagueness of Lindsey's "two or three like / two page

TABLE 5.5.
Different Descriptions of Specific Papers

| Stza | Lindsey's Narrative (1) | Blia's Narrative (2) | Stza |
|------|-------------------------|----------------------|------|
| 1.3  | 11 LINDSEY: =[and we    | 51 BLIA:    and then we had | 2.4 |
|      | 12    the second semester | 52    our senior science project | |
|      | 13    we wrote probably like | 53    which is like | |
|      |       two or three like | 54    um | |
|      | 14    two page papers like | 55    a college | |
|      | 15    the first semester | 56    graduate research level | |
|      |                         |       sort of thing | |
|      |                         | 57    yeah | |

papers like" (Stanza 1.3, Lines 13–14) stands in contrast to the specificity of Blia's "senior science project." In both of these stanzas, we see Ochs and Capps' (2001) dimension of "tellability" coming into play. Both women situate their experiences as extremes set against an imagined, more moderate "norm" of what people experience in terms of high school writing. Lindsey only wrote "two or three like / two page papers" her first semester, whereas Blia had to go above and beyond the average high school student's effort as she compares her work to that of a college graduate research project. These extremes thus rate their stories as more "tellable" (in contrast to a more mundane activity or experience). In Stanzas 1.4 and 2.5, Lindsey and Blia provide further details about these experiences (see Table 5.6).

These two stanzas are the climactic moments of both of these narratives. In Stanza 1.4, Lindsey describes the second semester of her college prep class entirely using passive constructions. Her stresses on "whole" and "entire," as well as her repetition of "whole last semester" (Line 16),

TABLE 5.6.
Different Rating of Paper Writing Experiences

| Stza | Lindsey's Narrative (1) | Blia's Narrative (2) | Stza |
|---|---|---|---|
| 1.4 | 16 LINDSEY: and then the <u>whole</u> last semester | 58 BLIA: I had to do a | 2.5 |
| | 17     the <u>entire</u> last semester | 59     <u>experiment</u> | |
| | 18     was spent on writing a five page | 60     uh | |
| | | 61     find all the research that I like | |
| | 19     double spaced paper | 62     you know | |
| | 20 CHOUA: huh [the whole last semester | 63     background information I need | |
| | 21 BLIA:     [oh my | 64     analyze all the experiment data that I | |
| | 22 LINDSEY: the whole last semester | 65     got off my experiment | |
| | 23 CHOUA: I'm so (mad at) you guys | 66     <u>present</u> it | |
| | | 67     in a | |
| | | 68     uh | |
| | | 69     like | |
| | | 70     uh | |
| | | 71     format | |
| | | 72     like | |
| | | 73     some people used overhead I used | |
| | | 74     Power Point and | |

"entire last semester" (Line 17), and "whole last semester" (Line 22) suggest that she wants to emphasize her lack of activity over that time period, rather than any actual effort. There are no personal pronouns or characters mentioned, and the only verbs are passive: "*was spent* on *writing*" (Lines 17-18, italics added).

In Stanza 2.5, Blia does precisely the opposite. She focuses instead on the work she did and the effort it involved. Casting herself as the primary actor, Blia performs an experiment, finds the research, analyzes experiment data, and presents it. In addition, toward the end of the stanza, she positions herself in relation to other classmates who chose to present their work on "overheads." Unlike them, Blia used the computer program PowerPoint, a more technologically complex presentation mode than an overhead. So we see Blia emphasizing how much work she's done and offering a lot of evidence of what that work was like. In addition, by positioning herself alongside other peers at her high school, she begins to set herself apart from them. Contrast this to Stanzas 1.1, 1.4, and 2.1, where both Lindsey and Blia cast their high school experience in terms of "we." But in Stanza 2.5, Blia shifts to using "I": She doesn't say, "We had to . . . ," but instead emphasizes what "I" did. It is possible that everyone at her school went through the same process, but Blia doesn't explicitly say that. Note also that in Stanza 2.6 (see Table 5.7), Lindsey responds to Blia's account with, "[we didn't do <u>any</u>thing like that" (Line 79)—again, maintaining the position of herself *and* other members of her high school. Now, let's take a look at how Lindsey and Blia close off their narratives.

TABLE 5.7.
Different Narrative Closings

| Stza | Lindsey's Narrative (1) | | Blia's Narrative (2) | Stza |
|---|---|---|---|---|
| 1.5 | 24 | LINDSEY: (*inaudible*) but anyway I was like | 75 BLIA: it was a competition | 2.6 |
| | | | 76    it was so hard (*laughs*) | |
| | 25 | that was my college prep class | 77 LINDSEY: oh my <u>god</u>= | |
| | | | 78 BLIA   [so hard | |
| | 26 | BLIA:    [oh my god | 79 LINDSEY   =[we didn't do | |
| | 27 | LINDSEY: [so | <u>any</u>thing like that | |
| | 28 | CHOUA: hhh | | |
| | 29 | LINDSEY: yeah | | |
| | 30 | CHOUA: [it's so weird that | | |
| | 31 | BLIA:    [wow | | |
| | 32 | CHOUA:   [it's (???) | | |

Stanzas 1.5 and 2.6 operate as "codas" (Labov, 1972; Labov & Waletzky, 1997), which signal a return from the narrative frame space back to the present moment. For instance, when Lindsey says, "That was my college prep class" (Stanza 1.5, Line 25), she indicates that she has finished telling about her experience and opens the floor for her peers to respond, back in the present moment. Blia closes off her narrative by evaluating it: "It was so hard" (Line 76); "[so hard" (Line 78). Again, the distinction is telling. Blia emphasizes her difficulty and effort, seen in that she opens and closes her narrative with work: "We went through so much trouble (too)" (Stanza 2.1, Line 33); "It was so hard / / so hard" (Stanza 2.6, Lines 75, 78). In contrast, Lindsey returns to the event of her class, making little mention of the work she has done. In these narratives, Lindsey has chosen to foreground her lack of activity, whereas Blia has chosen to emphasize the amount of work she did.

In these two narratives, then, Blia constructs an image of herself as a hard-working student who met heavy demands made on her in terms of writing, and Lindsey portrays herself as a student who never had demands made on her in terms of writing yet, despite this lack, successfully accomplishes her academic goals (a theme that becomes especially prominent in Narrative 3). These self-constructions are reinforced by the relationships signaled to others within these narratives. Lindsey, in not naming or elaborating any other actors in her narrative, shapes a highly independent self, whereas Blia locates herself in the midst of performances that are influenced by other actors and participants. However, note that Blia asserts her independence by describing her efforts in her senior science project as her own work and by setting herself off from high school peers, whereas Lindsey does not distinguish her writing experiences from those of other students at her high school. So, although Lindsey does not name other independent actors, she positions herself within a collective group of students who shared the same high school writing activities. These self-other relationships are particularly germane as we consider how Lindsey, in Narrative 3, works to explain some of the differences she perceives between herself and Blia.

## Evaluating Positions: Using Markers to Explain Difference

Narrative 3 (re-presented below) details Lindsey's high school and her subsequent enrollment at Midwestern University. In many ways, this narrative can be read as an evaluation of the differences displayed in Narratives 1 and 2. Upon hearing Blia's account, Lindsey provides some additional information about her own high school, saying, "I graduated from a class of 36 though" (Line 80), showing what she believes is likely a marker of difference, suggested by her use of the word "though": the size of her school. But when Blia says, "(well) mine was like 40 / 40 / something" (Lines 82–84), Blia identifies with the marker Lindsey has just put out there. As a result, the "marker of difference" that Lindsey has just suggested has become less a marker of difference than a point of alignment. In response, Lindsey seeks an additional identifier, querying Blia, "what / was it private" (Lines 86–87). When Blia confirms that she did attend a private school (Lines 88–89), Lindsey goes on to say, "okay ours was definitely public" (Line 90) and describes her school further. Take a look at Narrative 3 with the stanza breakdown in Table 5.8.

TABLE 5.8.
Marking Difference

| Stza | | | Narrative 3: "I Don't Know How I Ended Up Here" |
|---|---|---|---|
| 3.1 | 80 | LINDSEY: | I graduated from a class of 36 though |
| Abstract | 81 | BLIA: | oh I had |
| | 82 | | (well) mine was like 40 |
| | 83 | | 40 |
| | 84 | | something |
| 3.2 | 85 | LINDSEY: | yeah ours was like |
| Complicating | 86 | | what |
| State | 87 | | was it private |
| | 88 | BLIA: | yeah |
| | 89 | | it's private |
| | 90 | LINDSEY: | okay ours was definitely public |
| | 91 | BLIA: | Oh |
| 3.3 | 92 | LINDSEY: | we had |
| Elaboration | 93 | | like |
| of | 94 | | kindergarten through 12 all in one building |
| complicating | 95 | | like |
| state | 96 | STUDENT: | (laughing) |
| | 97 | LINDSEY: | we were out in the boonies= |
| | 98 | BLIA: | [(laughs) |
| | 99 | LINDSEY: | =[never did anything |
| | 100 | | ever |
| 3.4 | 101 | | I don't know how I ended up here |
| Evaluation/ | 102 | | no idea |
| Coda | 103 | | but it's |
| | 104 | | it's worth it |
| | 105 | BLIA: | yeah |

Note that each stanza is labeled according to the function it plays in the story. Stanza 3.1 is an abstract, which provides an overview of the point of the story. Remember that as Lindsey begins to tell this narrative, she does not know what Blia will say in response, so we can read her initial utterance as offering a potential explanation for the difference between their high school experiences—Lindsey went to a small high school that did not have the same resources that presumably Blia's high school might have had. However, Blia responds by identifying with (not differentiating herself from) the small high school marker that Lindsey has just displayed. So in Stanza 3.2, Lindsey introduces a complicating state—"what / was it private" (Lines 86–87)—and explains that her high school was "definitely public" (Line 90), making more complex the relationships between the two schools and experiences. Now, instead of just two women having different high school experiences, we have a woman from a small public high school comparing her experiences with a woman from a small private high school. In Stanza 3.3, Lindsey elaborates on that complicating state, talking more about the physical size and relative isolation of her school. Then, in Stanza 3.4, she offers an evaluation of that experience while moving back into the present time frame.

Now, let's spend a bit of time thinking about how differences have been displayed and taken up over the course of these three narratives in light of the information revealed in Narrative 3. Two explicit discussions of difference have taken place over these three narratives: one in Narratives 1 and 2, which positioned two "extreme" academic experiences (cast in the guise of how much writing the women did during high school), and a second in Narrative 3, comparing characteristics of Blia and Lindsey's high schools. That is, factors communicating information to Blia and Lindsey within these narratives deal with their past encounters with writing in school: their academic work, the size of the school, and its public or private status. But beyond simply noticing and responding to markers of difference, Blia and Lindsey are enacting a complex dynamic of identification and differentiation through these narratives.

When Blia identifies with Lindsey's "small high school" experience, this identification is not taken up by Lindsey. Instead, she responds by finding ways to differentiate herself from Blia, as when she interrupts Line 85 to ask Blia whether she attended a private school. Although Lindsey may be trying to explain why her high school experience was so different from Blia's, why does she choose to focus on what distinguishes herself from Blia? It may be that, for Lindsey, Blia's high school description does not "fit" what she has previously known about small, public high schools. In this way, Lindsey's stance toward Blia can be characterized as relatively closed: She is not eager to "learn about" Blia's experience as much as she is eager to position herself and Blia in a particular way through the telling of this narrative.

Indeed, Lindsey's narrative is not just about situating Blia's narrative within Lindsey's frame of reference: It is also about being able to tell *her own* story, a story about her rise from "the boonies" and her arrival at Midwestern. It is here that the ethical implications of narrative positioning become especially clear. Because Lindsey's response to Blia does not offer Blia the space to construct herself further, but rather suggests a relatively fixed understanding of "small public" versus "small private" high schools, the worldview being established is more closed than open. Lindsey seems to already know what the experiences being revealed mean. She does not ask Blia questions about her high school experience; instead, she is ready to evaluate it. In fact, neither woman's story opens up the floor for further discussion of difference or reevaluation of past experience.

When teachers pay attention to students' narratives, it is worthwhile to consider how much freedom narratives provide for self- and other constructions. What are some of the ways in which narratives construct others (as characters in stories) or position others (in relation to stories being told)? Narrative 3 suggests the import that such positioning can have: Blia's attempt to identify with Lindsey is shut down when Lindsey calls on the public nature of her high school: "okay, ours was definitely public" (90). The public nature of Lindsey's high school allows Lindsey to maintain the separation she needs to finish constructing the self she wants to display. Blia's experience is no longer relevant, or invited, within this frame. Lindsey's talk in Narrative 3 suggests that even as narratives can often invite other narratives and talk (e.g., seen in the way Narrative 1 "invites" the sharing of other experiences, as Blia does in Narrative 2), they can also shut down conversation, particularly if others are positioned in ways they do not want to be or their experiences are framed as irrelevant or unimportant.

Although I have suggested here that Narrative 3 shows Lindsey constructing a particular self, and working to differentiate herself from Blia, simply documenting the positions she establishes does not fully explain what is happening during this interaction. As I noted earlier, markers are displayed in a variety of different ways: Verbal utterances are only one such source.

## THERE'S MORE TO THE STORY!
## LIMITATIONS OF NARRATIVE ANALYSIS

In the last section, I discussed some of the ethical dimensions of narrative analysis in terms of how narratives *respond* to others and position others. Another ethical dimension to consider is what we are leaving out by focusing our analysis on spoken narratives. There are other markers of difference that are never openly discussed by either Blia or Lindsey but that still frame their interaction. Both Blia and Lindsey (as do all face-to-face interactants) *embody* markers of difference that convey information about who they are, how they affiliate, and how they respond to one another. So before even initiating conversation with one another, they are processing information about one another—for instance, the color and length of their hair, the shape and color of their eyes, their skin coloring, the clothing they wear, even their names—that influences the differences they are likely to engage (or *not* engage).

More extensive analysis of other ethnographic data (e.g., field notes, videotaped interactions, observation of the two women in other contexts, examination of other narratives they tell) would enrich this narrative analysis, providing more evidence for particular claims and perhaps deeper understanding of how physical and spatial arrangements influence narrative tellings. Narrative analysis, although offering a rich resource for teachers seeking to cultivate responsible and responsive ties with others in their classrooms, does not tell the whole story. Dialogic narrative analyses can (and should) be fruitfully combined with other analytic strategies and data sources.

The embodiment of markers makes the work of displaying and describing difference particularly challenging because physical markers are often not explicitly named or discussed in talk. This is where developing a language for talking about difference becomes particularly crucial. It is only by engaging a back-and-forth conversation about and between interpersonal interactions and categories used to name difference that broad descriptors such as White, Asian American, woman, English speaker, and so on can be seen as flexible and dynamic terms.

## IMPLICATIONS
## FOR TEACHER EDUCATION

If schools, according to Gee (1996), "ought to allow students to juxtapose diverse Discourses to each other so that they can understand them at a meta-level through a more encompassing language of reflection" (p. 190), then narrative analysis and attention to the creation of selves in language is one step toward this activity. Although Gee is focused on enabling students to see discourses positioned alongside one another, I believe this claim can be similarly applied to juxtaposing narrative tellings to better understand difference. Thus, I want to encourage teachers and teacher educators to attend to the ways that narrative structures provide space for the examination of differences among students, as well as between teacher and students.

My arguments here dovetail with the voices of educational researchers, such as Dyson (1997a) and Rex, Murnen, Hobbs, and McEachen (2002), who have argued for the importance of listening to students and teachers across a wide spectrum of voices. To better understand how this listening happens, I have examined mechanisms for *coming to know* others by attending to narratives told in classroom contexts. Such coming to know presumes a beginning stance that does not take for granted one's knowledge and that involves an openness to examining assumptions and initial reactions. Schultz (2003) elaborates one such form of openness through her articulation of "listening across difference." Through this frame, Schultz illustrates how learning to listen involves cultivating an openness to difference: "If teachers assume they do not know what is behind students' utterances or their performances in school, then learning about who their students are and what they bring from communities can shift understandings about them, expanding possibilities for learning" (p. 79).

Schultz's work in some respects responds to issues identified by Gomez, Walker, and Page (2000) with regard to narrative knowledge-making. As Gomez et al. noted in their study, prospective teachers' narratives, rather than setting experience up for critical reexamination, mainly served to "author identities that reinscribed their personal experience as guidelines for how to teach others" (p. 742). This parochialism, however well intentioned, reflects an orientation to difference that privileges affiliation and knowing about others, rather than a sensitivity to the *lack* of knowledge we have about others. The question of *how* such knowledge is generated on an interactional level within classrooms remains a persistent issue for teachers who may feel overwhelmed by the incredible range of experiences, knowledges, and linguistic resources that students bring with them into the classroom. In response, I have tried to show how examining narrative knowledge-making can facilitate this bridging of worldviews and differences by employing a comparative method through which teachers can identify and engage markers of difference.

Indeed, one of the primary benefits of such narrative analysis is that it facilitates the identification of markers of difference and how they are deployed. It is important for teachers not simply to identify markers that distinguish them from their students but to attend to the ways that such markers bear meaning among themselves and their students. As we see in Lindsey's response to Blia, the way markers are taken up and responded to may mean the difference between bringing a student into an inclusive classroom environment and pushing that student aside. How do we, as teachers, construct identifications and differentiations with our students? How do those positions matter? How do we hold ourselves *responsible* for the positions we take?

Taking into consideration the analysis displayed in this chapter, encouraging teachers to ask how markers of difference are deployed as they engage with their students is a first step toward cultivating an awareness of their positioning and of their students. I hope these analyses have suggested some ways of learning from students how best to teach them, and through this, to see the possibilities available within classrooms as spaces where students and teachers are learning from and with one another.

Questions for Reflection:

1. Tape-record yourself one day in class and listen for examples of your own narrative-telling. Write down the story as accurately as you can, keeping as close as possible to your actual words. What kind of story did you tell? Who populated it? How did it relate to your educational/classroom goals? Who responded to the story? In what ways?
2. How do your stories open up spaces (or act as models) for particular ways of being and doing in your classroom? How might you purposefully craft such narratives with an eye toward inclusivity and ethical responsibility?
3. How do the stories you share in your classrooms position you with regard to others—be they students, teachers, or teacher educators?
4. How do your students communicate their ways of knowing through narrative?
5. What are some ways that you can invite students' attention to their own and others' narratives?
6. One key difficulty with engaging difference is precisely that one does not know difference until one encounters it. What are some ways that you can prepare yourself to authentically respond to the incredible range of experiences and identities shown among your students?

## NOTES

1. For a useful discussion of interculturality as situational and emergent (rather than defined by the cultural identities of the people involved in an interaction), see Mori (2003).
2. The closest we can come is to what Bakhtin (1981) calls "aesthetic activity," the act of empathizing with the Other. "I must put myself in his place and then, after returning to my own place, 'fill in' this horizon through that excess of seeing which opens out from this, my own, place outside him" (p. 25). Such aesthetic activity involves a commitment to the Other, a commitment to difference, to understanding how and in what ways we are noncoincident.
3. See also Bauman (1986) on the distinction between narrative events and narrated events.

# REFERENCES

Bakhtin, M. M. (1981). *The dialogic imagination: Four essays* (M. Holquist, Ed.; C. Emerson & M. Holquist, Trans.). Austin: University of Texas Press. (Original work published 1935)

Bakhtin, M. M. (1990). *Art and answerability* (V. Liapunov & K. Brostrom, Trans.). Austin: University of Texas Press.

Bakhtin, M. M. (1993). *Toward a philosophy of the act* (V. Liapunov & M. Holquist, Eds.; V. Liapunov, Trans.). Austin: University of Texas Press.

Bamberg, M. (1997). Positioning between structure and performance. *Journal of Narrative and Life History, 7*(1–4), 335–342.

Bauman, R. (2004). *A world of others' words: Cross cultural perspectives on intertextuality.* Malden, MA: Blackwell.

Bialostosky, D. (1999). Bakhtin's "rough draft": Toward a philosophy of the act, ethics, and composition studies. *Rhetoric Review, 18*(1), 6–23.

Dyson, A. (1997a). *What difference does difference make? Teacher reflections on diversity, literacy, and the urban primary school.* Urbana, IL: National Council of Teachers of English.

Dyson, A. (1997b). *Writing superheroes: Contemporary childhood, popular culture, and classroom literacy.* New York: Teachers College Press.

Dyson, A. (2003). *The brothers and the sisters learn to write: Popular literacies in childhood and school cultures.* New York: Teachers College Press.

Gee, J. P. (1996). *Social linguistics and literacies: Ideology in discourses* (2nd ed.). Philadelphia, PA: Falmer Press.

Gomez, M. L., Walker, A. B., & Page, M. L. (2000). Personal knowledge as a guide to teaching. *Teaching and Teacher Education, 16*(7), 731–747.

Gumperz, J. (1992). Contextualization and understanding. In A. Duranti & C. Goodwin (Eds.), *Rethinking context* (pp. 229–252). New York: Cambridge University Press.

Halasek, K. (1999). *A pedagogy of possibility: Bakhtinian perspectives on composition studies.* Carbondale: Southern Illinois University Press.

Heath, S. B. (1983). *Ways with words: Language, life, and work in communities and classrooms.* Cambridge, UK: Cambridge University Press.

Hicks, D. (1996). Learning as a prosaic act. *Mind, Culture, and Activity, 3*(2), 102–118.

Hicks, D. (2000). Self and other in Bakhtin's early philosophical essays: Prelude to a theory of prose consciousness. *Mind, Culture, and Activity, 7*(3), 227–242.

Holland, D., Lachiotte, W., Skinner, D., & Cain, C. (1998). *Identity and agency in cultural worlds.* Cambridge, MA: Harvard University Press.

Hull, G., & Schultz, K. (2002). Literacy and learning out of school: A review of theory and research. *Review of Educational Research, 71*(4), 575–611.

Juzwik, M. M. (2004). Towards an ethics of answerability: Reconsidering dialogism in sociocultural literacy research. *College Composition and Communication, 55*(3), 536–567.

Kerschbaum, S. (2005). *Beyond simple inclusion: Towards engagement with difference in a postsecondary writing classroom.* Unpublished doctoral dissertation, University of Wisconsin-Madison.

Labov, W. (1972). *Language in the inner city: Studies in the Black English vernacular.* Philadelphia: University of Pennsylvania Press.

Labov, W., & Waletzky, J. (1997). Narrative analysis: Oral versions of personal experience. In J. Helm (Ed.), *Essays on the verbal and visual arts: Proceedings of the 1966 annual spring meeting of the American Ethnological Society* (pp. 12–44). Seattle: University of Washington Press. (Original work published 1967)

Louwerse, M. M., & Mitchell, H. H. (2003). Toward a taxonomy of a set of discourse markers in dialog: A theoretical and computational linguistic account. *Discourse Processes, 35*(3), 199–239.

Mori, J. (2003). The construction of interculturality: A study of initial encounters between Japanese and American students. *Research on Language and Social Interaction, 36*(2), 143–184.

Ochs, E., & Capps, L. (2001). *Living narrative: Creating lives in everyday storytelling.* Cambridge, MA: Harvard University Press.

Purcell-Gates, V. (1997). *Other people's words: The cycle of low literacy.* Cambridge, MA: Harvard University Press.

Rex, L. A., Murnen, T., Hobbs, J., & McEachen, D. (2002). Teachers' pedagogical stories and the shaping of classroom participation: "The Dancer" and "Graveyard Shift at the 7-11." *American Educational Research Journal, 39*(3), 765–796.

Schiffrin, D. (1987). *Discourse markers.* Cambridge, UK: Cambridge University Press.

Schultz, K. (2003). *Listening: A framework for teaching across differences.* New York: Teachers College Press.

Wilkerson, W. S. (2000). Is there something you need to tell me? Coming out and the ambiguity of experience. In P. Moya & M. Hames-Garcia (Eds.), *Reclaiming identity: Realist theory and the predicament of postmodernism* (pp. 251–278). Berkeley: University of California Press.

Wortham, S. (2000). Interactional positioning and narrative self-construction. *Narrative Inquiry, 10*(1), 157–184.

# 6

# EXPLORING CULTURAL COMPLEXITY IN TEACHER EDUCATION THROUGH INTERACTIONAL AND CRITICAL STUDY OF CLASSROOM NARRATIVES

*Mary M. Juzwik*

Ever since encountering the work of Shirley Brice Heath (1983) as an early career English teacher on the Navajo reservation, I have sought out ways to better understand and respond to the complexities of culture in classroom life. Now, as a teacher educator, I seek out ways to help teachers explore culture in practically grounded, yet theoretically nuanced ways. In my teacher education work, I have often asked myself: How can students and I together move beyond recognition of surface dimensions of culture (e.g., food, festivals, etc.) to a deep appreciation for the myriad and complex cultural practices that students figuratively "bring along" with them to the classroom and the ways that cultural meanings emerge, interact with, and transform one another in classroom life? Some of the more complex and often obscured dimensions of culture that I struggle to bring to the fore in my work with teachers include, for example, how groups and nations construe history in contested processes, how religious and other deeply held beliefs shape interpretations of language and literature, how multiple heritages can conflict both within and among individuals, and how family practices can transmit and transform knowledge and practice across generations.

To address this pedagogical dilemma, I have turned to sociolinguistic narrative analysis. Several years ago, I decided to use the study of oral classroom narrative—based on my work as a researcher—to deepen conversations about the complexities of culture in my teacher education classroom. What follows is an account of how this effort played out and what I learned from meditating retrospectively on the experience. Grounded in the story of this pedagogical experiment, I aim to show that examining narrative data from classroom research can be a powerful tool for teaching and learning about culture in teacher education. However, this process can open up challenging moral complexities that are part of encountering cultural difference and taking it seriously.

## COMPLICATING CULTURE: WHAT I WANT TEACHERS TO LEARN AND WHY NARRATIVE ANALYSIS HELPED TO ACCOMPLISH THIS LEARNING

Certain commonsense notions of culture, *static* views, seem to saturate educational conversations about students. After outlining some of these notions, I present an alternative *emergent* approach to understanding culture. It is this latter way of seeing, hearing, and experiencing culture that I am working toward in my teacher education efforts. Finally, I lay the groundwork for the teacher education context in which I sought to engage students in grappling with the complexities of culture.

### What Is Culture?

Culture is sometimes seen as a "thing" that students bring along with them to school and this thing—rather like the lens of a mistaken eyeglass prescription—exerts a negative impact on their learning and achievement. I am going to refer to this as a "static" view of culture. From this perspective, one's culture is determined by and relatively unchanging within one's location or participation in a particular group (e.g., rural Appalachian, Polish immigrant, or urban African American). Individuals belong to (usually one) culture in which they are more or less "competent" (Hymes, 1972). When taking such a view of culture, insights about language and learning (usually deficiencies in one or both of these areas) are tied to and explained in terms of one's membership in that particular group. This view of culture comes into play, for example, when educators assume that students' cultural backgrounds create deficits that must be overcome or eradicated in the interest of academic achievement. This view of culture is perhaps most egregiously on display in schools when days, weeks, or months are set aside to celebrate obvious and easily stereotyped dimensions of culture, such as foods, festivals, music, and national language variation—surface manifestations of culture that Derman-Sparks (1989) aptly called a "tourist curriculum." A tendency here is to exoticize and reify "other" cultures. Although this notion of culture has been outdated in the anthropological literature for some time (e.g., Duranti, 1997), it lingers on in educational conversations about teachers and students. I aim to move teachers beyond such reductive tourist conceptions of how culture works—and *can* work—in the classroom.

Just as others (such as Heath) opened my early career teaching eyes to new ways of understanding culture and teaching, so I seek to introduce teachers to alternative, more dynamic, and more imaginative ways of understanding culture and classroom life. How do people accomplish things with available cultural resources, which can involve a great range of "stuff" (as linguist James Gee likes to call it) such as language and other symbolic resources, money and other economic resources, and material items? How do they move—sometimes with grace, sometimes with great conflict—among various networks of cultural practice? These questions lie at the core of an *emergent* approach to culture (Rosaldo, 1989; Sarris, 1992; Tedlock & Mannheim, 1995). This more "actor-centered" approach focuses on how culture is dynamically shaped through differentially valued networks of practice and through individuals' negotiation and appropriation of systems of participation within such networks.[1]

Most parents know all too well that students' cultural worlds do not remain unchanged when they come to school. Although certainly children and youth do bring certain cultural resources along with them into the classroom, interactions with others and with the official and hidden curriculum of schools interact with, transform, and complicate those cultural resources (e.g., Sarris, 1992). Literacy researcher Anne Haas Dyson (2003) calls these complicated cultural processes "recontextualization." Rather than being dupes of any one cultural world (including the system of school), children and youth are inventive and create new meanings with the range of cultural resources and cultural networks available to them. Teachers who understand and capitalize on this complexity—those with *saberes* or "social wisdom," as Poveda (2002) put it—can exert enormous influence as they invite culturally diverse children to participate in, influence and transform, and deeply learn from classroom lessons and practices.

However, the cultural negotiations in classrooms are just as often fraught with conflict. Educator and public intellectual Richard Rodriguez's (1982) powerful autobiographical narrative offers but one example. The story dramatically illustrates the potentially devastating identity and motivational consequences for students, including himself as a youngster, who learned *in school* to be ashamed of their family's cultural ways. Ethnographer Greg Sarris (1992) likewise documents how students on the Kashaya Pomo reservation in California revolted from the well-intentioned, yet culturally simplistic, efforts of their young, white, progressive teacher to introduce a seemingly "culturally relevant" text about Slug Woman. Because Slug Woman was a powerful and fearful figure in many of the students' families' oral storytelling traditions, students wanted nothing to do with the insipid prose of the text, the content of the Slug Woman story, and their teacher. The lesson was a disaster because the teacher failed to appreciate or successfully navigate the complexities of culture in her teaching situation.

Because of the potential for harm in the cultural navigation and negotiation taking place in classrooms, teachers need tools for apprehending and acting on the cultural complexities they encounter therein.

## Teaching Context

Although the question of how to engage teachers in understanding culture in meaningful and complex ways is an abiding concern in my teacher education work, I here chronicle a particular mini-unit that took place in a course I taught during the spring of 2004. I was teaching a junior-level course about "language and literacy" that was part of a teacher education program at a public university in the southwestern United States. The 28 teacher candidates enrolled in the class were mostly juniors, with a few sophomores. They were a diverse group of folks reflecting the diversity of the university. Several women in the class were adult nontraditional college students with deep roots in the surrounding communities. One middle-aged Hopi woman aimed to teach students on the Hopi Nation after obtaining her degree. Several who lived in rural areas commuted a considerable distance to campus. One young man was on the football team. Several were the first in their families to attend college. This diverse group of teacher candidates, of whom I was exceedingly fond, was hungry to learn and eagerly took on new challenges.

During the mini-unit about culture, we explored the dilemmas of how to navigate cultural difference in the classroom. As part of this short unit, we read various texts chosen to present complicated, emergent notions of culture. We read the already introduced article by Greg Sarris. We also read an article by researchers Norma Gonzalez and Luis Moll (1995), which introduced the idea of students' "funds of knowledge," the pedagogical possibilities of making "home visits," and what it might mean for teachers to develop an "anthropological imagination." As part of this unit, a group also guided the class through a series of activities explicating major themes from Heath's (1983) book, *Ways With Words*. It was against this backdrop of cultural study that I introduced narrative analysis.

## USING NARRATIVE ANALYSIS
## TO UNDERSTAND CULTURE AND THE CLASSROOM

### Why Narrative Analysis?

Why use narrative analysis to deepen and concretize our study of culture and teaching? I realized that the emergent approach to culture in which I sought to engage my students can be quite abstract, particularly for those who have not had a life full of experiences encountering obvious cultural differences. Further, a hallmark of emergent approaches to culture is attention to language in use (or discourse). As many sociolinguists have observed, discourse can both shape and be shaped by social interaction in various discursive contexts (Gumperz, 1982; Hanks, 1996). Narrative, as a form of discourse, is one among many "cultural forms" through which meanings and identities are negotiated (Holland Lachicotte, Skinner, & Cain, 1998). The classroom can be an important site of narrative negotiation: In many contexts (although perhaps increasingly less so as students move up in the grades), oral and written narratives pervade classroom talk. Narrative practices can become such a familiar part of classroom life that they come to seem "natural" or normal" to tellers and listeners (Rex et al., 2002).

Studying classroom narratives—stories that teachers and students told every day as part of their classroom interactions—offered a way to help teachers see culture-in-(inter)action through a defamiliarization process. A body of classroom-based research stimulated my thinking about this possibility. Work dating from the early 1980s chronicled children's narratives during sharing time and reading groups and the disadvantages certain groups of children—such as working-class African Americans—faced in these contexts (Cazden, 2001; Collins, 1996; Michaels, 1981; Michaels & Cazden, 1986). More recent research on narrative interactions in primary classrooms, for example, literacy researcher David Poveda's (2002) study, suggested that teachers with cultural wisdom could scaffold children's narrative storytelling to support their participation and learning.

With all this in mind, I reasoned that narratives could provide a way to study how individuals located themselves culturally through stories they tell, used specific cultural resources in telling narratives, and negotiated a variety of cultural worlds. In short, narrative offered a powerful tool for defamiliarizing cultural practices and making *culture*—as a focal concept—seem commonplace and everyday rather than exotic or other.

## Resources for Sociolinguistic Narrative Study in Teacher Education

How do teacher educators get into narrative analysis? What resources are available for use? In Chapter 3 of this volume, Rymes and Wortham introduce certain key linguistic concepts underlying sociolinguistic narrative analysis. In what follows, I highlight crucial sociolinguistic strategies used for narrative analysis with teachers and a second set of critical questions about teaching and teacher education.

### Linguistic Strategies

A first step in studying oral narrative data involves using audio, video, or other recording devices to capture precise articulations and uses of language in context. Therefore, to study narrative with teachers, it is necessary to capture everyday narrative language in the classroom (or other relevant) context to serve as an analytic focus. Although I had recorded the narrative talk I introduced to teacher candidates for a book project I was working on at the time (Juzwik, 2009), it can also be highly productive for teachers to record talk in their own classrooms or in classrooms where they are observing. This option can, however, raise issues around confidentiality that should be addressed.

After recording narrative data, the first analytical step is transcription. Narrative researchers (e.g., Mishler, 1991) convincingly show that how narrative is transcribed matters a great deal for the interpretations to be made from the narrative. For this reason, teacher educators and teachers may wish to experiment with different modes of transcribing. For example, I used what narrative researchers call a "performative" transcription method as part of my research (Juzwik, 2006; Scollon & Scollon, 1981; Tedlock, 1983), and I used these transcriptions for my work with the teachers. This notation system entails laying out narratives a bit like poetry, with each line a breath unit—that is, words uttered in between even the faintest of pauses (see also Kerschbaum, chap. 5, this volume). Transcribing in this manner has the effect of showing lots of white space on the page, like poetry, which can speed up the reading to simulate the experience of the narrative talk. Also like poetry, the narratives are divided into stanzas according to thematic or episodic criteria (for more on this, see Juzwik, 2004). This sort of transcription offers one powerful way to see the poetic dimensions of narrative that were discussed by Rymes and Wortham (chap. 3, this volume).

In preparation for class (but not as part of my research project), I also did some analytical work with the data. Because I wanted to have a more open-ended conversation about the narrative data, I did not make this

analysis explicit to students. However, it developed my own understanding of the narratives as cultural forms in the classroom. I compared a student and a teacher narrative, which I introduce later, along the five
dimensions introduced in Chapter 3 by Rymes and Wortham: tellership,
tellability, embeddedness, linearity, and moral stance. This work allowed
me to dig into the narrative data from an emergent cultural perspective:
to understand narratives as doing social and international work in the
here and now of the classroom, rather than only representing the past
events of the Second World War and the Holocaust.

*Critical Questioning*

Beyond these linguistic strategies, a second set of tools involves critical questioning about teaching and teacher education. Similar to the
questioning strategies proposed in Freire's (1994) pedagogy, critical questioning about narrative can move sociolinguistic narrative study square-
ly into the realm of teacher education. Teachers and teacher educators can
pose critical and defamiliarizing questions about the cultural functions—
and the attendant pedagogical possibilities and problems—of oral narrative discourse in classrooms. Such questions are driven by "Why?",
"What if?", "What more would we need to know?", and similar explorations of possibility and critique.

Teacher educators can invent and pose questions around the educa-
tive opportunities that might be opened up in the classroom through particular narratives. We can also invent and pose questions around opportunities potentially closed down or "miseducative" opportunities opened
up through the cultural complexities of narrative tellings. For example,
sometimes teachers telling stories from their own lives can shut down
student conversation and participation (Caughlan, 2004). The narratives
introduced in previous chapters, the narratives I introduce next, or narratives recorded and transcribed by teachers can be used as texts for such
questioning processes.

## DATA: TWO NARRATIVES ABOUT THE HOLOCAUST

### Introducing the Data

As already mentioned, the two narratives stem from my narrative study
of the rhetorical dimensions of teaching about the Holocaust and the
Second World War (see Juzwik [2009] for more details about the context of
that study). In summary, the study took place in a combined seventh- and
eighth-grade classroom in a small midwestern city during a 6-week elective unit about the Holocaust taught during December 1999 and January

2000. At the time of the study, the teacher, Jane Connor (pseudonym), was a 25-year-old non-Jewish woman in her third year of teaching. In what follows, I introduce one of Jane's narratives and one student narrative.

Because these stories are disturbing, and because they are necessarily decontextualized from the flow of classroom talk, I ask readers to withhold judgment of the teacher and her handling of the content. Because narrativization of this content can be troubling and complex, and has been a matter of enormous scholarly debate (e.g., Lang, 1990), I hope to complicate judgments about the teacher's talk. With this comparison, I aim to illuminate how oral narratives in classroom talk—especially narratives about troubling and at times silenced subjects such as the Holocaust and the Second World War (see Perl, 2005)—can be sites to investigate and teach about cultural complexity and difference.

Jane told the first narrative about midway through the unit,[2] during a lesson about *Kristallnacht*, "the night of broken glass," which occurred on November 9, 1938. On this night, German officials and citizens destroyed Jewish businesses and synagogues.

### Narrative 1. Violence Was the Way to Go (1/5/00)

1. I mean,
2. A lot of horrible things have happened
3. Before 1938,
4. To be sure.

5. But this was
6. A gov-ern-ment policy
7. Where
8. Not that we're just going to call you not-civilians,
9. No that we're just gonna say
10. You're Jews
11. Where you're gonna have to wear badges.

12. But now,
13. We're gonna destroy everything you own,
14. We're gonna beat you up,
15. We're going to burn your synagogues.

16. This was a violent act to the extreme,

17. And no one stepped up and said,
18. All right,
19. We've had enough,
20. You've done all this,

21. We can't let you do any more.
22. This kind of showed him
23. That violence was the way to go,
24. Or can be the way to go,
25. Because no one's going to stand up
26. And say it's wrong.

27. They haven't to this point,
28. And they're not going to
29. Even when violence is incorporated.

30. They're just going to walk on their merry way,
31. And ignore the whole thing
32. As much as they can.

The second narrative was uttered by a student, Nathan, who brought to the class a complex cultural identification in relation to the course content of the Holocaust. I did not, however, collect elaborate data about his family's story nor did Nathan consent to be interviewed as a "focal participant" in my project (although he did consent to be a participant in the research). As this narrative indicates, he had German relatives (on one side of his family) who were involved in Nazi perpetrations of atrocity. However, on the other side of his family tree was a Jewish grandmother in Austria who fled to the United States in the 1930s to escape Hitler's genocide (a story he also shared with the class, not long after sharing the following narrative). In this classroom, Nathan's family's storylines about the Second World War interacted with the curriculum about the Holocaust. Comparing Jane's and Nathan's narratives reveals how exceedingly different cultural storylines about the Nazi genocide were articulated, negotiated, and contested. I follow some transcription conventions detailed in Kerschbaum (chap. 5, this volume, Table 5.1).

*Narrative 2. Taking Part in a Public Beating (1/13/00)*

Nathan:
1. He uh
2. told me that
3. he had to take part in
4. a public
5. beating?

Jane: your great uncle?
Nathan:      yeah
Jane: (had to take part in it?). Okay?

6. It was like part of his training.

Jane: Huh

7. And
8. He was almost kicked out[3]
9. Because he didn't want to do that.
10. So they basically
11. Forced him
12. To beat the guy.

Jane: Was it, who wa-, was it a Jewish person, or was [it just, another enemy?
Nathan:                                                                [yeah, it was a Jewish
                                                                         person

Jane: Like it was a Jewish person. From the town or whatever? I mean, was it?

13. It
14. It was like,
15. He was already captured

Jane: okay ((very softly))

16. And
17. he said,
18. It was
19. It was like a disgrace
20. To beat the guy.
21. Because he was like
22. skinny
23. And

Jane: Mm hmm.

24. Like basically
25. All bones.

Jane: Mm hmm

26. So he didn't really want to do it.
27. But he was forced to.

Jane: Do you have any idea of like time periods for any of these things?

28. Well,
29. I know my
30. Uncle
31. He was too young

32. to actually become an SS trooper,

Jane: 'Kay ((softly))

33. So he just basically stayed in training.
34. And my grandpa
35. Fought basically
36. Like, half the war.

Jane: Okay. Alright. So the uncle who had to do the beating, d-, h-, do you think it was during the war when he had to do that public beating? Or do you think it was before the war?

Nathan: I think it was probably at the beginning.

Jane: Okay. So, might have been. I'm trying to figure out who the Jewish guy would have been. Just, probably just a citizen, and not a ghetto, prisoner, or anything else. Probably just a normal citizen who hadn't yet been transferred. Alright, interesting. So your grandparents, at least on one side, are from Germany?

## Reading Narrative Events as Emergent Cultural Processes

To prepare myself for the narrative work with teachers, I compared Jane's and Nathan's narratives according to tellership, tellability, embeddedness, linearity, and moral stance—a set of linguistic resources that may seem technical and distant from teacher education. However, this work forms an important backdrop for considering these two particular narratives as *emergent cultural processes* in the life of this particular classroom. This comparison sets the scene for my pedagogical use of the narratives.

## Tellership

Is a narrative told by a single teller or co-told by multiple tellers? In this respect, I noticed a striking difference between the two narratives. Jane's narrative was "monologic," told by a single teller uninterruptedly holding the floor. Nathan's narrative, however, was dialogically co-constructed. Jane prompted Nathan's narrative through questions (e.g., "your great uncle?") and comments (e.g., "huh" and "okay"), which seemed to serve two functions. First, Jane's speech cues showed that she was an engaged listener. Second, she scaffolded Nathan's emerging narrative, leading to a more fully developed narrative than was likely to have been uttered without this support. This is a familiar sort of pedagogic conversation often held between adults and children in many Western contexts, especially when adults are trying to lead children in particular directions or to specific conclusions (cf. Ochs & Capps, 2001). Nathan had already shared this story with the teacher, so that these questions were not "authentic," in the sense of the asker not knowing the answer (Nystrand, 1997). I found the role and direction of the teacher questioning particularly interesting with respect to moral stance-taking discussed later.

## Tellability

How reportable, or newsworthy, is a narrative telling? "Violence Was the Way to Go" was newsworthy as part of Jane's curriculum: She chose to dramatize the course content of *Kristallnacht* to show why this was such an important event in the unfolding events of the Holocaust and the Second World War. Jane seemed to perform this and other narratives in her teaching about the Holocaust to counteract the potentially "dry" data of timelines and note-taking (much of which was presented in a lecture mode, with students taking notes). Narratives appeared to be a way for Jane to "spice up" potentially dull historical material. Through contrast of what Nazis did and what nobody did (i.e., stand up and talk back to Hitler's atrocity), Jane showed how history might have turned out otherwise. Thus, the narrative took a perspective critical not only of Nazi perpetrators but also of bystanders who stood by passively (who "went along their merry ways") in response to these horrors. Nathan's narrative, in contrast, told a family member's firsthand experience with the horrors of the Holocaust. Unlike the perspective of the teacher narrative, this story took a sympathetic perspective on Nazi perpetrators, showing that they were people, too, with feelings and constraints on their action.

## Embeddedness

Is a narrative relatively detached or embedded in surrounding talk? Jane's narrative was detached from surrounding discourse through various framing and stylistic choices that set the narrative apart from the surrounding talk. Poetic devices included repetition, contrast, rhetorical schemes and tropes, and syntactic patterning (see Juzwik [2004] for more details). Jane also employed theatrical language, including "constructed dialogue" (Tannen, 1989), where she quoted (or made up) the words of others, for example, in Line 10 and Lines 18–21. Expressive intonation was another dramatic way that Jane aesthetically detached her narrative telling from the surrounding talk. The single tellership also served to detach the narrative telling, making it more "performative" than Nathan's, which is to say the narrative put Jane on display and at the center of attention.

Nathan's narrative, in contrast, was embedded in a conversation with Jane, his teacher. This embedding was multilayered, as Nathan's narrative utterance here in class was embedded in prior conversations with Jane, in which he shared some of his family's story. In this immediate narrative talk, the thread of the narrative was woven through student narration and teacher responses that seemed to spur on more narration. As discussed in the prior section, this narrative was "dialogic" in the sense that it was constituted through interaction between two people. The distinction between the detached teacher narrative and the embedded student narrative may be shaped by the cultural norms of classroom behavior. It is also possible that Jane possesses more competence in constructing and telling narratives than does Nathan, who is much younger and has had less time to develop this skill.

## Linearity

How does the plot, the sequencing of events in time, move forward in a narrative? What events in the past were recounted and which were not? What is the significance of the particular ordering of past events? Examining the linearity of narrative draws attention to both the temporal and causal ordering of events.

Both narratives contained a relatively closed temporal and causal ordering of events. In Jane's narrative, a closed temporal ordering consisted of the following events and nonevent:

1. Prior events = horrible things happened (e.g., Jews wearing yellow stars and having citizenship taken away by Nazis) (Lines 8–11);
2. Event 1 = NOW: an unprecedented horror because it was a government policy that wrought violence on persons, their belongings, and their places of worship (Lines 12–15);
3. Nonevent 2 = no public outcry from German people and church (Lines 16–21);
4. Event 3 = Hitler was shown that "violence was the way to go" (Lines 22–26).

Nathan organized his narrative around the follow temporal/causal sequencing:

1. Event 1 = Nathan's great uncle was almost kicked out of Nazi training because he didn't want to beat someone (Lines 8–9);
2. Event 2 = He beat a skinny fellow to avoid being kicked out of training (Lines 10–12);

3. Event 3 = He feels that it was a disgrace to beat such a defenseless person (Lines 16–20).

In both of these narratives, the events were represented in the (presumed) order in which they occurred in time (although the "feeling of disgrace" in the third event of Nathan's narrative may well have pervaded his great uncle's experience of the entire incident). Moreover, the causal linkages between events were "closed" in the narration, rather than being subject to multiple interpretations and open-ended exploration of possible causal relationships. Perhaps the historical and vicarious content of these stories (i.e., they recount events that happened to others, rather than to the tellers), including the disturbing topic of atrocity and the Nazi genocide, made more open-ended exploration difficult.

## Moral Stance

Moral stance is a particularly salient dimension of narrative tellings for cultural consideration: What is the point of a story? Is the evaluative point of the narrative—its "so what?"—certain and constant or uncertain and fluid? What kinds of persons is the storyteller presenting (both herself and others)? What kind of world is the storyteller portraying? In the context of teaching about historical events and analyzing vicarious narratives, moral stance-taking offers a rich analytic lens for considering how *cultural differences* emerge through narrative tellings. In the teacher narrative, Jane staked a strongly critical, certain, and constant moral stance of condemnation, one that is fairly consonant with a well-rehearsed storyline of the Nazi genocide in the United States (Novick, 1999). She critiqued both perpetrators of *Kristallnacht* and those who did not "speak up" in protest (namely, the church and the German people). There also was a possible implied moral lesson for students to glean from this narrative: They—unlike the Nazi and German bystander anti-heroes—should be the kinds of heroes who would stand up and say, "All right, we've had enough—You've done all this, we can't let you do any more" in the face of such a "violent act to the extreme."

The student narrative, in contrast, focused on Nathan's great uncle not wanting to participate in violence but being forced to do it anyway, a circumstance that mitigated his responsibility for his actions. Nathan seemed to be trying to humanize—perhaps even to justify—the participation of Germans (i.e., his family) in such brutal activities. The paraphrased repetition of Lines 7–12 ("And/He was almost kicked out/Because he didn't want to do that./So they basically/Forced him/To beat the guy") and Lines 26–27 ("So he didn't really want to do it./But he was forced to") made the moral stance of the narrative seem consistent—

even certain throughout the narrative. Jane did not, however, take up this point in her responses to Nathan's telling. Instead, she expressed more interest in how the details fit into the historic timeline of the events of the war. On one plausible reading, she shied away from exploring or encouraging Nathan to elaborate this particular moral and cultural perspective on Nazi atrocities. Through her line of questioning, Jane effectively closed down one avenue for possible development in Nathan's narrative. She also had the final word in this narrative event, which probably had the effect of further burying Nathan's moral stance.

Thus, reading narratives culturally offers insights into individuals' particular, culturally situated interpretation of the world and the people in it. By examining moral stance, it became possible to consider cultural differences emerging across evaluative stances in different narrative tellings.

## Introducing the Narratives to Teachers

With this preliminary groundwork laid, I introduced the narratives to the teacher candidates in my class. I prepared photocopies of the transcribed narratives and distributed them to the class. I verbally provided a little bit of context about the teacher and Nathan and that classroom context, about as much as provided in this chapter. Working in small groups, the teacher candidates closely read and discussed these narrative examples guided by two focal questions:

1. How is culture entering the classroom through these two oral narratives?
2. Can your group derive any "lessons for teachers" from this comparison? (Lesson plan, 3/25/04)

## INSIGHTS AND QUESTIONS: PROBING POSSIBILITIES FOR THE USE OF NARRATIVE ANALYSIS TO CULTIVATE CULTURALLY WISE TEACHERS

In response to this activity, in concert with the prior readings and discussion, teacher candidates and I generated several descriptive insights about how we could see culture in teaching through narrative study. My presentation of these insights is not a report of results of empirical teacher research. Rather, this account is constructed from my notes in class, from my memory of the activity and interaction, and from my subsequent meditation on what I learned as a teacher educator through that experience. Critical questioning allowed me to further probe and reflect on these claims about the uses of narrative as emergent cultural process in classroom talk. Each of the following sections uses the teacher education classroom experience as a starting point to critically question each of the propositions about narrative generated in my pedagogy.

## 1. Narrative Study Can Make Visible the "Invisible" Dimensions of Culture in Classrooms

The first proposition is basic: Study of transcribed classroom narratives can reveal to prospective teacher educators some of the "invisible" dimensions of culture in classrooms. For example, Euro-American students and teachers come to their classrooms with cultural heritages and family stories, just as Navajo and Hopi students and teachers come to their classrooms with rich cultural heritages. Although this insight may be obvious to more experienced teachers or teacher educators or to those who have felt the stings of being made "other" because of their culture or skin color, this is a point that pre-service teachers (many of whom are white middle-class women) need to consider and explore in multiple ways.

In discussing this theme, I shared with the teacher candidates the cultural complexities of my own experience as an early career teacher on the Navajo reservation. As a Euro-American woman who had grown up in small-town northern Ohio, my cultural resources were invisible to me. A freshly minted teacher from a conservative midwestern institution beginning my career in a fifth- and sixth-grade classroom, I lacked the tools to see the complexities of my own cultural training and positioning even while I understood "Navajo culture" as a fascinating (even exotic) culture to which I had little access and about which I knew very little. Undoubtedly naïve, but quite desperate to learn how to be a competent teacher in the small community where I taught, I set out to learn all that I could about the lives of my students and their families through home visits and other community activities. Despite these attempts, I still lacked the necessary tools to see my own cultural contribution to the classroom practices and how these intersected with the Navajo cultural ways that students brought into the classroom.

As we discussed how culture can be more or less visible (to ourselves and others), I contrasted my early lack of cultural understanding with a more recent insight gained in conversation with a Navajo woman selling jewelry. She showed me a necklace with an image of a stalk of corn and began to explain the spiritual and life-giving significance of corn in her Navajo heritage, in her words, "to our people." This prompted me to think about the meaning of a stalk of corn to "my people": From the frame of reference of my midwestern upbringing, "corn-on-the-cob" (as we called it) evoked harvests from the family garden, picnic suppers with family and church members, and long humid summer evenings. We did not attach a spiritual significance to corn. In fact, my Christian parents and their friends would likely have labeled such a practice "animism." Nonetheless, corn did hold cultural meaning for me and "my people."

I introduced the comparative narrative data from Jane and Nathan and also shared this autobiographical lore believing that this insight— that important aspects of classroom culture are "invisible" and can be rendered more "visible" through narrative study—is important for teacher candidates. The different moral stances articulated in Jane's narrative and Nathan's narrative hint at the particularly critical importance of this insight for those teaching in or preparing to teach in classrooms populated by students whose cultural heritages differ from their own. It is also critical in classrooms confronting disturbing subjects such as the Holocaust.

However, the promise of making cultural and cultural practices and moral stances visible through narrative comes with some attendant risks that should also be critically considered. Sociolinguist Dell Hymes (1996) argues that narratives operate as a "restricted code" for speakers and listeners (Bernstein, 1971). This means that the alignments and positionings of speaker and audience are taken for granted, as are many of the contextual factors necessary to make meaning of the story. A prior analysis of the structure of Jane's narrative highlighted how a "fully formed narrative" can implicitly deliver a great deal of moral content (Juzwik, 2004; Labov, 1972). Gee (1985) points out, however, the problems that artful narrative styles can create for children when they enter school and their white middle-class teachers do not understand or value their ways with words. Another scenario is also possible: students not understanding or valuing their teacher's narrative style(s). The linguistic, ethnic, racial, and religious makeup of classrooms may influence students' or teachers' reception of narrative discourse. It is conceivable that narrative language (because so much is *not* stated explicitly in this discourse genre) could cause conflict or marginalization in diverse classrooms where few cultural patterns, beliefs, or customs are shared.

These possibilities suggest the following critical questions for teachers and teacher educators to ask of narrative discourse:

- What assumptions about "the way the world is" are at work in this narrative? What assumptions about "the way the world should be" can be discerned?
- What forms of language are used by the teller? What forms of language are not present? (This last question is much easier to answer in comparative analysis across different classrooms and different speakers.)

- Are these assumptions and language forms shared by every-one in the classroom? What kind of information would be needed to answer this question?
- What is a scenario in which Jane's narrative could have been used to marginalize a student? What is a scenario in which this narrative could have been used to encourage "identifica-tion" with course content?

By asking such questions, I believe, it becomes possible to explore how narratives can reinforce stereotypes and further marginalize those who are "other" or "different" in our classrooms.

## 2. Narrative Study Can Show How Moral Perspectives on Curricular Materials Differ Along Ethnic, Religious, or National Heritage; Family Heritage; and/or an Individual's Double or Multiple Heritages.

Different moral perspectives on the Holocaust, and on other curricular materials (such as culturally relevant literature), may relate to diverse family, ethnic, religious, or national cultural heritages. With the case of teaching about the Holocaust, educational researcher Simone Schweber (2004a) documented pervasive differences in what counts as knowing and learning about the Holocaust in different contexts of public educa-tion. Other studies showed dramatic differences in learning about the Holocaust across religious schools, for example, a fundamentalist Christian school and an orthodox Jewish girls school (Schweber, 2004b; Schweber & Irwin, 2003). In one Christian school (Schweber & Irwin, 2003), the primary text was Corie Ten Boom's (2009) *The Hiding Place*.[4] In this book, the focal character is a Christian woman who helped Jews and was sent to a concentration camp for these actions. The particular experi-ences of Jews—as a group, unlike Christians, targeted for unprecedented state-sponsored systematic annihilation—were effaced altogether in this curriculum. In the Orthodox Jewish context, by contrast, the unique posi-tion of Jews as targets of total systematic annihilation was an important focus (Schweber, 2004b).

Even within a shared religious or ethnic collective heritage, there is likely to be variability in the stories students' families tell about the Second World War and the Holocaust. Additionally, pre-service teachers can profit from recognizing that, as Nathan's example demonstrates, stu-dents sometimes enter classrooms with doubled, multiple, and some-times conflicting heritages that may enter into curricular conversations.

This second proposition raises a complicated issue: What is to be the "unit of analysis" in teaching and learning about cultural difference through narrative study or more generally? Embedded in this statement are durable "macrostructures" that might account for cultural difference (e.g., ethnicity, religion, nation). I label these categories "macro" because they exist over a relatively large group of people and "durable" because they persist over time and space. However, we might notice the "micro" dimensions of culture when we look at an individual as an intersecting point of cultural difference or in linguistic terms when we look at a single narrative utterance as a cultural hybrid. Negotiating the macro- and micro-aspects of narrative analysis in teacher education, as in educational research, is no small challenge. Going too far in the "macro" direction runs the risk of gross stereotypes and overgeneralization or essentialization about a group of "others." The potentially negative consequences of "othering" Jews in this way through Holocaust education are vast and alarming given the persistence of anti-Semitism. Going too far in the "micro" direction, however, we risk losing the explanatory power of theorizing culture in classrooms altogether.

Rich potential for learning about culture through narrative rests in the dynamic movement between the microlanguage of narrative emerging in the here and now and the broader cultural and historical storylines indexed, challenged, or interactionally emergent through classroom talk. Some critical questions to guide this negotiation are these:

- What questions might be further explored about Nathan, his family, his great-uncle, and German people in the 1930s, 1940s, and so on to further understand his great-uncle's moral stance in the narrated scenario?
- What words or patterns of language in this narrative could be indexed to cultural affiliation (at any level)?
- What are the advantages and drawbacks of conceptualizing culture and cultural difference in classrooms at each of these different levels: Ethnic group? Religion? Nation? Family? Individual?
- Think of a specific teaching context in which one of these "units of analyses" would seem most generative. Why would it be so productive?

## 3. Teacher and Student Narratives Are Sites Where the Intersections of Cultures in Classrooms Can Be Probed.

Teacher and student narratives are one site where the "intersections" of cultures in classrooms (both within and among classroom participants) can be explored. Because of this, it could be possible for teachers to consciously use students' narrative tellings as opportunities to conversationally explore the multiplicity of possibilities and alternatives embedded in any given narrative or to openly, tentatively, and collaboratively articulate possible alternative narratives around a given situation.

Nathan's narrative, for example, could invite further inquiry into the possible reasons why everyday people—such as Nathan's great uncle—could have been induced to participate in atrocity. Yet teachers must be careful with such inquiry because Nathan's position was tenuous and heritage-wise he was caught in the middle of competing storylines about the Holocaust. Because we may well have such students in our classrooms, it is wise to proceed cautiously—with deep respect for all that we do not know about students and their families—in doing such narrative analytic work. Questions raised by student narratives, at least in elective courses such as the one in which these narratives occurred, could be used as generative guides for future inquiry. Another pedagogical possibility is for teachers to prompt students to imagine other narrative scenarios through hypothetical "what if?" questions. For example, "What if Nathan's great-uncle had refused to participate in this beating?" or "What if the person Nathan's great-uncle was commanded to beat were in top health, would it have been less of a disgrace?" Here again, such hypothetical explorations would need to be pursued cautiously, with a teacher remaining attuned to how Nathan responded. Such exploration of student and teacher narratives holds the potential to lead to deepened understandings of the cultural complexities of interpreting the past.

While "grappling with narrative" may encourage students and teachers to gain experience with and cultivate respect for cultural difference, it is also important to confront the possibility of "othering" or treating narrative as expressive of a stable unchanging cultural reality. The treatment of Jews as a cultural group in Jane's narrative hints at this problem because Jews are not narrated as subjects or "agents" in Jane's or Nathan's stories. Critically questioning the intersections of culture in classrooms can be framed as an exploration of the possibility for harm to individual class members or to cultural groups through narrative tellings.

Furthermore, if the idea of the classroom as a site of cultural "intersection" is not treated robustly, we risk the possibility of students becoming overly self-focused or celebratory of "who I am." An extreme kind of cultural relativism ("Everyone is different and that's okay") could result in either excessive navel-gazing or exoticizing "other" cultural groups (such as I did with Navajos early in my teaching career), rather than critically considering the complex challenges offered by diverse classrooms.

Perhaps more daunting is the possibility that teachers and teacher educators might stumble on some "hot lava" topics (Florio-Ruane, 2001) in doing the kind of exploratory questioning and response that I proposed earlier. I think, for example, of the heated reception that surrounded Daniel Goldhagen's (1997) historical study, *Hitler's Willing*

*Executioners*, which explored why everyday Germans (e.g., soldiers and policemen) were willing to go along with the Nazi genocide. I witnessed one forum about this book at the University of Colorado in the late 1990s that ended in tears and shouting. Critiques of the book also proliferate on the Internet. The reception of Goldhagen's book illustrates the potential for controversy about the very topic and questions I proposed (above) to explore around Nathan's narrative. Because they are personal or "personalized" through narrative form, there is no guarantee that such exploration about the Holocaust (or other culturally complex topics) will not raise uncomfortable—even explosive—responses.

Four critical questions can help teachers explore narratives as intersections of cultures and values:

- In Jane's narrative, how are Jews made "other" through language patterning? What stereotypes about Jews might such portrayal promote in classrooms?
- What are some other points of view through which the events recounted in these narratives (Jane's and Nathan's) might be told? Who might have a different storyline to report on these narrated events? How might the narrative go differently if told from this other vantage point?
- What challenges do teachers and peers face in responding to (or interactionally guiding) a narrative telling such as Nathan's? What other "ways with words" might a teacher use to respond? What might a teacher say to prompt responses from other students?
- Are there some culturally or personally "loaded" narrative topics that should not be explored or pursued in the classroom? What are some scenarios where narrative tellings or explorations might open cultural conflicts that are "too hot to handle"?

## 4. Stories Generate Stories, Potentially Opening Intercultural Dialogues.

Examining these stories with teacher candidates elicited stories from them and from me—a discourse pattern colleagues and I have elsewhere called "conversational narrative discussion" (Juzwik, Nystrand, Kelly, & Sherry, 2008; cf. Johnson, 2005). Narrative opened a dialogue with the potential to represent and transform cultural understandings. This observation comports with what narrative theorists have noted about the generative powers of narrative (Ochs & Capps, 2001). I already discussed the narratives of personal experience that I shared with students, elaborating my own cultural disorientation and naivete as a new teacher. In conversational response to these comparative narratives about the Holocaust, I recall Ginny recounting how when German tourists come to the trading post in her reservation community (not infrequently), everyone asked them about the Holocaust and little else.

These examples suggest the invitational dimensions of narrative discourse, a mode that may invite teachers to imagine other possible worlds than their own. Conversational narrative discussion may also invite teachers to respond to these imagined worlds from their own individual positions—their "once-occurrent" moment of being, as Bakhtin (1990, 1993) put it (Kerschbaum, chap. 5, this volume). Although narrative tellings in classrooms are inevitably culturally and individually variant, cross-cultural studies have shown that narratives are a powerful universal form through which humans around the world make sense of experience (cf. Ochs & Capps, 2001).

Just as stories can invite more stories, however, stories can also shut down subsequent stories and responses. For example, a skilled and powerful storyteller can mesmerize an audience, inviting evaluation, delight, awe, terror, and many responses other than more stories. I witnessed such a response to a powerful storyteller when a distinguished senior professor visited my class to discuss her book with students who had just finished reading it. A hush fell over the classroom as she spoke, and students later reported being so "in awe" in her presence that they were afraid to speak up in response. Other students reported that her presentation was so "mesmerizing" that they could not think of a single thing to say. Similar observations have been empirically documented in systematic research on classroom discourse. For example, Samantha Caughlan (2004) found in a classroom discourse study that teachers sometimes used narrative as a discourse strategy for "leaving," rather than "inviting," classroom discussions about literature.

Narrative spells and conversational narrative discussions may make some students uncomfortable. Several years ago, I observed a classroom in which one middle-school boy, when his classroom got into a conversational narrative discussion having to do with sex, shifted awkwardly and asked the teacher, "How'd we get onto *this* topic?!?" In contrast, others may feel so comfortable narrating personal stories that teacher educators need a psychoanalyst or counselor to manage, for example, sharing about a rape or "coming out" for the first time. Critical questions to consider about the generative powers of story include the following:

- How do we handle the possibility of too many stories in the classroom? How might teachers misuse the pleasurable dimensions of storytelling? What criteria might we use to determine how much story is too much story?

- Under what conditions might "story generate story"? Under what conditions might narratives close down responses?
- How do teachers set appropriate boundaries on classroom storytelling practices without being overly controlling (see previous section on teacher authority)?

## CONCLUSION

My teaching story suggests that when framed as (a) a linguistic resource for observing and understanding the complexities of cultural difference in classrooms, and (b) a tool for critically questioning what to do about these complexities, sociolinguistic narrative study has the potential to become a powerful tool for teaching and learning about culture in teacher education. I do not believe that teacher educators need to become linguists to guide teachers in doing this kind of work, although certain interpretive strategies from linguistics can certainly be helpful. As our work with these brief narratives shows, even brief excerpts of narrative talk in classrooms can be plumbed through multilayered interpretation and can raise tremendously complex and puzzling problems of practice. The task for teacher educators is to dig deeply into the narrative data, whatever it may be.

This work also involves posing and welcoming the challenging moral questions raised when conducting narrative analysis of classroom life. Part of the process is resisting quick judgments and simplistic moral condemnations of others' errors and encouraging a willingness to explore multiple interpretive possibilities. Other teacher educators and scholars have observed the power of *literary* narratives to cultivate teachers' cultural and moral imaginations (Coles, 1990; Florio-Ruane, 2001). The chapters in this volume further suggest that *oral* narrative analysis in teacher education may also prove a useful pedagogy for promoting morally engaged—what Stephanie Kerschbaum might call *answerable*—encounters with cultural difference.

## NOTES

1. I do not discuss this working distinction between "static" and "emergent" approaches to culture in great detail because of my current focus on pedagogical concerns within teacher education. My understanding of culture is participationist, a general theory of culture that aligns with Rex's introductory discussion of participation in classrooms (Chapter 1, this volume). Duranti (1997) usefully lays out how understanding culture in terms of participation can be distinguished from other contemporary theories of culture, including the more

cultural psychological orientations (e.g., Rogoff, 1990; Vygotsky, 1978, 1986; Wertsch, 1985) so often invoked in educational writing about culture (see especially Duranti, 1997, pp. 23–50, 280–333). Theorizing culture through a focus on how face-to-face interactions unfold, how systems of participation are structured in specific activity contexts (e.g., classrooms), and how different systems of participation are differentially valued within broader fields of social practice (e.g., Bourdieu, 1991) aligns with research traditions focused on the study of language-in-use, including sociolinguistics and linguistic anthropology (cf. Jaworski & Coupland, 2006).

2. I contextualize and analyze this narrative in greater detail elsewhere (Juzwik, 2004).
3. I interpret Nathan to mean that his great-uncle was almost "kicked out" of the Nazi training program of which he was part (pre-SS).
4. This book was also used as part of my own introduction to the Holocaust in eighth-grade social studies in the 1980s, also in an evangelical Christian school. However, my teacher—the indefatigable Jim Gale—did not use Ten Boom's book exclusively: He also read aloud to the class Elie Wiesel's *Night*, a book deeply rooted in Jewish religious experience.

## REFERENCES

Bakhtin, M. M. (1990). *Art and answerability: Early philosophical essays by M. Bakhtin* (V. Liapunov & K. Brostrom, Trans). Austin: University of Texas Press. (Original work published 1919–1986)

Bakhtin, M. M. (1993). *Toward a philosophy of the act* (Vadim Liapunov, Trans.; V. Liapunov & M. Holquist, Eds.). Austin: University of Texas Press.

Bernstein, B. (1971). *Class, codes, and control* (Vol. 1). London: Routledge.

Boon, C. T., with Sherrill, E. & Sherrill, J. *The hiding place.* Peabody, MA: Hendrickson Publishers.

Bourdieu, P. (1991). *Language as symbolic practice.* Cambridge, MA: Harvard University Press.

Caughlan, S. B. (2004, December). *The dialogic dance of discussion.* Paper presented at the annual meeting of the National Reading Conference, San Antonio, TX.

Cazden, C. (2001). *The language of teaching and learning* (2nd ed.). Portsmouth, NH: Heinemann.

Coles, R. (1990). *The call of stories: Teaching and the moral imagination.* New York: Houghton Mifflin.

Collins, J. (1996). Socialization to text: Structure and contradiction in schooled literacy. In M. Silverstein & G. Urban (Eds.), *Natural histories of discourse* (pp. 203–228). Chicago: University of Chicago Press.

Derman-Sparks, L. (1989). *Anti-bias curriculum: Tools for empowering young children.* Washington, DC: National Association for the Education of Young Children.

Duranti, A. (1997). *Linguistic anthropology.* Cambridge, UK: Cambridge University Press.

Dyson, A. H. (2003). *The brothers and sisters learn to write: Popular literacies in childhood and school cultures.* New York: Teachers College Press.

Florio-Ruane, S. (2001). *Teacher education and the cultural imagination: Autobiography, conversation, and narrative.* Mahwah, NJ: Lawrence Erlbaum Associates.

Freire, P. (1994). *Education for critical consciousness.* New York: Continuum.

Gee, J. (1985). The narrativization of experience in the oral style. *Journal of Education, 167*(1), 9–35.

Goldhagen, D. (1997). *Hitler's willing executioners.* New York: Vintage.

Gonzalez, N., & Moll, L. (1995). Funds of knowledge for teaching in Latino households. *Urban Education, 29,* 443–470.

Gumperz, J. (1982). *Discourse processes.* Cambridge, UK: Cambridge University Press.

Hanks, W. (1996). *Language and communicative practices.* Boulder, CO: Westview Press.

Heath, S. B. (1983). *Ways with words: Language, life, and work in communities and classrooms.* Cambridge, UK: Cambridge University Press.

Holland, D., Lachicotte, W., Skinner, D., & Cain, C. (1998). *Identity and agency in cultural worlds.* Cambridge, MA: Harvard University Press.

Hymes, D. (1972). On communicative competence. In J. B. Pride & J. Holmes (Eds.), *Sociolinguistics* (pp. 269–293). London: Penguin.

Hymes, D. (1996). *Ethnography, linguistics, narrative inequality: Toward an understanding of voice.* London: Taylor & Francis.

Jaworski, A., & Coupland, N. (2006). Introduction. In A. Jaworski & N. Coupland (Eds.), *The discourse reader* (2nd ed., pp. 1–37). London: Routledge.

Johnson, A. (2005). *Towards a dialogic approach to teachers' narratives.* Unpublished doctoral dissertation, University of Wisconsin, Madison, WI.

Juzwik, M. M. (2004). What rhetoric can contribute to an ethnopoetics of narrative performance in teaching: The significance of parallelism in one teacher's narrative. *Linguistics and Education, 15*(4), 359–386.

Juzwik, M. M. (2006). Performing curriculum: Building ethos through narrative in pedagogical discourse. *Teachers College Record, 108*(4), 489–528.

Juzwik, M. M. (2009). *The rhetoric of teaching: Understanding the dynamics of Holocaust narratives in an English classroom.* Cresskill, NJ: Hampton Press.

Juzwik, M. M., Nystrand, M., Kelly, S., & Sherry, M. (2008). Oral narratives as dialogic resources for classroom literature study: A contextualized case study of conversational narrative discussion. *American Educational Research Journal, 45*(4), 1111–1154.

Labov, W. (1972). The transformation of experience in narrative syntax. In W. Labov (Ed.), *Language in the inner city: Studies in the Black English vernacular* (pp. 354–396). Philadelphia: University of Pennsylvania Press.

Lang, B. (1990). *Act and idea in the Nazi genocide.* Albany: State University of New York Press.

Michaels, S. (1981). Sharing time: Children's narrative styles and differential access to literacy. *Language in Society, 10,* 423–442.

Michaels, S., & Cazden, C. (1986). Teacher–child collaboration as oral preparation for literacy. In B. Schieffelin (Ed.), *The acquisition of literacy: Ethnographic perspectives* (pp. 132–154). Norwood, NJ: Ablex.

Mishler, E. (1991). Representing discourse: The rhetoric of transcription. *Journal of Narrative and Life History, 1*(4), 255–280.

Novick, P. (1999). *The Holocaust in American life*. Boston: Houghton Mifflin.

Nystrand, M., with Gamoran, A., Kachur, R., & Prendergast, C. (1997). *Opening dialogue: Understanding the dynamics of language and learning in the English classroom*. New York: Teachers College Press.

Ochs, E., & Capps, L. (2001). *Living narrative: Creating lives in everyday storytelling*. Cambridge, MA: Harvard University Press.

Perl, S. (2005). *On Austrian soil: Teaching those I was taught to hate*. Albany: SUNY Press.

Poveda, D. (2002). Quico's story: An ethnopoetic analysis of a Gypsy boy's narratives at school. *Text, 22*(2), 269–300.

Rex, L. A., Murnen, T. J., Hobbs, J., & McEachen, D. (2002). Teachers' pedagogical stories and the shaping of classroom participation: "The Dancer" and "Graveyard Shift at the 7-11." *American Educational Research Journal, 39*(3), 765–796.

Rodriguez, R. (1982). *Hunger of memory: The education of Richard Rodriguez*. New York: Bantam.

Rogoff, B. (1990). *Apprenticeship in thinking*. New York: Oxford University Press.

Rosaldo, R. (1989). *Culture and truth: The remaking of social analysis*. Boston: Beacon.

Sarris, G. (1992). Keeping slug woman alive: The challenge of reading in a reservation classroom. In J. Boyarin (Ed.), *The ethnography of reading* (pp. 238–269). Berkeley: University of California Press.

Schweber, S. (2004a). *Making sense of the Holocaust: Lessons from classroom practice*. New York: Teachers College Press.

Schweber, S. (2004b, December). *Blackened lines: Learning about the Holocaust in a girls' Yeshiva*. Paper presented at the annual meeting of the Association for Jewish Studies, Chicago, IL.

Schweber, S., & Irwin, R. (2003). "Especially special": Learning about Jews in a fundamentalist Christian school. *Teachers College Record, 105*(9), 1693–1719.

Scollon, R., & Scollon, S. B. K. (1981). *Narrative, literacy and face in interethnic communication*. Norwood, NJ: Ablex.

Tannen, D. (1989). *Talking voices: Repetition, dialogue, and imagery in conversational discourse*. Cambridge, UK: Cambridge University Press.

Tedlock, D. (1983). *The spoken word and the work of interpretation*. Philadelphia: University of Pennsylvania Press.

Tedlock, D., & Mannheim, B. (Eds.). (1995). *The dialogic emergence of culture*. Urbana: University of Illinois Press.

Vygotsky, L. (1978). *Mind in society* (M. Cole, V. John-Steiner, S. Scribner, & E. Souberman, Eds.; A. Luria, M. Lopez-Morillas, & M. Cole, Trans.). Cambridge, MA: Harvard University Press. (Original work published 1935–1966)

Vygotsky, L. (1986). *Thought and language* (A. Kozulin, Trans.). New York: MIT Press. (Original work published 1934)

Wertsch, J. V. (1985). *Vygotsky and the social formation of mind*. Cambridge, MA: Harvard University Press.

# 7

# REFLECTIONS OF A CULTURAL TRANSLATOR

## Andrea Zellner

As a teacher of literature, I place value on the power of the story. But it must be remembered that literature does not exist in a vacuum. Indeed, it is often a powerful moment in the classroom when students recognize what exactly resonates with modern audiences to create a classic out of the story of an adulterous woman living in the colonies in *The Scarlet Letter* or the observations of a Midwesterner on the tragic consequences of hedonism in *The Great Gatsby*. As a teacher, I often find myself arguing for the value of these texts, especially in the face of the reluctance of my students to engage with them. It often seems that in "listening" to my classrooms, my students are telling different sorts of tales than F. Scott Fitzgerald and Nathaniel Hawthorne. When the culture of the common texts diverges from the culture of the classroom, I often become the mediator between the two. As a white, middle-class woman teaching prescribed texts in a classroom of African-American students, I become simultaneous ambassador and translator of the canon.

Recently in my classroom, during the study of *The Great Gatsby*, a text that, to put it mildly, does not historically excite and engage my students, one of my female students was intently reading. The book, however, was not the assigned text. The title, "Girls in Da Hood," was garnering interest from all the students nearby. They were engaged in a critical analysis of the characters, the quality of the writing, and the plausibility of the plot. Intrigued myself, I asked to see the book. Thus began a ritual of my reading of the text aloud and my students hooting in laughter at my "proper" pronunciations of the "hood" dialect that peppered the book. This point of intersection between what we *should* be reading and what my students were actually reading, this moment of listening and highlighting the culture differences between my students and me, represented the greater conflicts present in the classroom. Our stories are meaningful, and the ways we tell them are meaningful. I can remember, shortly after this incident, when I was listening to a student recount her recent interactions with another teacher that led to the student's suspension from school. As the student told her story, I found myself obsessively interjecting and correcting her vernacular:

Student: "It was mines."

Me:       "Mine."

Student: "Right, mine, so I says,"

Me:       "Said."

Student: "So I said, I ain't"

Me:       "I am not."

Student: "Ms. Zellner! I am never telling you a story again!"

And she was right—why should she tell me the story when I constantly interrupted the pace and power of her tale with the issue of Standard versus non-Standard English? When is it appropriate to correct a student's verbal grammar? This was a particular point of contention within the English department at my school. There were some who felt that it was not appropriate to "correct" a student's verbal departure from non-Standard English, whereas others considered it the highest form of teaching malpractice to refrain, even characterizing it as racist, believing that to refrain from that correction was to prevent that student's access to the "language of commerce." As a teacher, I had to negotiate these points of difference and decide my own path, my own moral stance, as Mary Juzwik describes, on the correcting of my students. As a white teacher, layered on top of this largely pedagogical discussion were implicit judgments about race and culture: As a teacher, I am correcting grammar, and as a white teacher I am judging the language of my students, who are reflecting the dialect of their communities, as "incorrect." Indeed, questioning my students' avoidance of Standard English is beyond the study of grammar and reflects whose language choices we value in the dominant culture. It is not an easy decision to correct their speech, and I can safely say that I was never comfortable verbally correcting my students' speech.

Czeslow Milosz states that "language is the only homeland." The mother tongue, the language of our mothers, the familiar, places each of the members of the classroom in a various positions. I was told as a pre-service teacher that "he who does the talking does the learning," and so I allowed my students to speak. As they did, I was forced to confront our differences in the most honest and loving ways possible.

When I stand up to guide my students through our American Literature curriculum, the very texts we are asked to read and examine are points of entry into whose stories are valued. The reason it was funny to my students that I read "Girls in Da Hood" aloud is that those stories are not valued in our curriculum. In fact, my little performance did little to dispel this idea: We were mocking the idea that the voices that mirrored the lives of my students had no place in the discourse of our classroom. Instead, we were examining the lives of the rich, white, and selfish of the 1920s. Each text chosen for our curriculum is a judgment on all the other texts not chosen: These stories by largely white, Euro-American men are more important than the myriad experiences of the other races, cultures, and genders that make up the American culture. It has long been lamented that the canon does not often recognize the scope of these experiences.

As a teacher, when such narrow experiences are presented in the name of "cultural literacy" and the "language of commerce," I become a cultural translator. Someone has to bridge the gap between the experiences and cultures of my students and the experiences and cultures presented to them in the canon. Thus, as an educator, I must also examine the ways in which I am different from my students and listen to the ways they identify themselves. As the Rosetta stone of culture, history, gender, race, and so on, I recognize my ethical responsibility to identify and celebrate the cultural identity of my students.

Before I can ethically engage in this way with my students, I feel it is important to examine my own judgments and moral stances. Before I ever step foot into the classroom, it is imperative that I unearth the innate ideas I hold about myself as a member of American society, as a woman, and as a person of European descent. These markers of difference, as Kerschbaum discusses, impact the identities of my students and can either value or devalue them.

I have come to believe in the sentiment that the reason we cannot move beyond racism in this country is because white people do not openly acknowledge their own racism, their own white privilege. To state that one holds racist beliefs is terrifying for most people, especially those who are Caucasian. Critical analyses of the ways in which pop culture reinforces racial stereotypes are easy to come by. More difficult to acknowledge are the ways in which white people have been conditioned to accept these stereotypes and the ways in which they perpetuate and enact these stereotypes. What it takes to be a good ambassador between the races is to be able to own and acknowledge the racism to which we have been inured since infancy. I am a racist. I have been habituated in my lifetime, through television, movies, and the opinions of my community, to see non-whites as "other," to judge others based on their skin color. It would be impossible to be raised in American society without these ideas worming their way into the collective psyche. As an educator, through the stories I tell about myself and others, I need to confront and uproot these conditioned responses to avoid the reactions detailed in the chapter—making the "other" culture exotic or refusing to see people in conflict, only as victims and perpetrators. I have to confront this dormant, underlying racism before I enter the doors of my classroom. Even in homogenous, all-white communities, I have to recognize and root out these ideas before I pass these judgments and ideas onto the children who sit in front of me, expecting to be educated.  I realized that, to be a racist, a homophobe, or a chauvinist, I do not have to consciously adopt the fears and prejudices those titles imply. When the dominant culture notices difference, it is usually with disdain or fear. To walk into my classroom, hoping to change the ways our society functions, hoping to empower the very people who have been marginalized by racism, gender bias, homophobia, class bias, and the like, I need to recognize the ways in which my privilege dominates my thinking and then cut it out. In this way, I can "authentically respond to the incredible range of experiences and identities" shown among my students, as Kerschbaum challenges me to do.

Through examining my own and my students' narratives, I can then recognize the insidiousness of the "isms." By naming and recognizing them, I can begin to change them, first in myself. Then I can move on to challenging them in others. This model, in turn, allows students to reorganize their own thinking while preserving the best of them. This process, through the crucible of the classroom, is what attracted me to the profession in the first place. Even if a teacher is not intending to teach for social justice, the canon requires this type of self-appraisal if only to avoid the scenarios that do not value the culture of my students. Juzwik's powerful example of Jane and Nathan illustrates the reason that, as teachers, we must be aware of the impact that narratives have on our students. We must move to the "emergent" understanding of culture to avoid teaching "malpractice." As we prepare to enter a classroom of students, each of whom has a different identity and culture, we must be able to recognize the power of those cultural narratives, value them without exoticizing them, and realize the explicit and implicit ways our own telling of narratives impacts our students.

Johnson discusses the need for examination of one's own personal narratives in pre-service teacher education. She states, "Part of urging teachers to engage critically with the racial, social, class, and gendered antecedents of these practices is encouraging them to consider their moral perspectives and how they give shape to their instructional choices." As teachers, we need to examine our privilege. To ignore the impact of the authority we hold as teachers, when students so often want to impress and please us as authority figures, holds consequences far beyond the four walls of the classroom. In the end, the shared experience of classroom learning impacts both teacher and student alike. Careful examination of our narratives, and the lessons we learn about others and ourselves from these narratives, can make this impact transformative to all who enter the classroom.

In the Introduction, Lesley Rex discusses the tensions between personal morals and professional ethics that can erupt. These tensions have been with me throughout my teaching career. To me, teaching a lesson with the idea that "every child can learn" means that the lesson will look a certain way: The physical space is arranged in a circle to encourage collaboration; I am equal to my students, more facilitator than pedagogue; the room is filled with the energy of new ideas. To a colleague, these same aspects signal chaos, poor classroom management, and students out of control. In teaching situations where professionals are desperate to impact student learning because the test scores are going down, the trend toward traditionalism prevails: students in rows, diagramming sentences, teacher as holder of all knowledge. I read this as fear: fear of failure, of losing our jobs, of losing the students. In the face of fear, each professional reexamines his or her personal teaching philosophy, sometimes leading to conflict. It is the way we choose to negotiate these conflicts that begins to define us educators. It is often difficult, the way fraught with hurt feelings and professional disagreement. I can't say I always negotiated these professional minefields with grace. I have found myself on the receiving end of the ire of my colleagues over a disagreement on the best way to improve students' grammar and mechanics. These are not trivial matters in a situation where we must all come to consensus in the best interest of the students. Those were the darkest days of my teaching career. However, recognizing the moral stances of my colleagues, seeing their true dedication to the students, reminded me that, although there may be disagreements, we are all focused on the students: guiding them to adulthood, giving them skills to succeed. More often than not, we all return to this common narrative: guiding, giving, cajoling, and teaching.

## ABOUT THE AUTHORS

*Stephen Bodnar* teaches language arts and Advanced Placement Psychology at Southfield-Lathrup High School in Southfield, Michigan. He received a doctorate in Curriculum & Instruction from Wayne State University and has taught writing extensively in college and high school. He is also a poet, his poems having appeared in *The MacGuffin, The Hemingway Review*, and many other publications.

*Amy Suzanne Johnson* is an Assistant Professor in the Language & Literacy program in the Department of Instruction and Teacher Education at the University of South Carolina. Her research program uses life history and ethnographic methods to examine individuals' literacy practices as they develop and change throughout their lifespans. Her research has been published in journals including *Journal of Teacher Education, Teaching and Teacher Education, Teachers and Teaching: Theory and Practice, The Reading Teacher, Journal of Adolescent and Adult Literacy,* and *English Education*. In 2007, she received the J. Michael Parker Award for Contributions to Adult Literacy from the National Reading Association; and in 2008 she was awarded the Promising Researcher Award from the National Council of Teachers of English.

*Mary M. Juzwik* is an associate professor of Language and Literacy in the College of Education at Michigan State University. She is affiliated with the Rhetoric, Writing, and American Cultures Program and the English department and is a principal investigator at the Literacy Achievement Research Center. Her current work focuses on classroom interaction in

English language arts classrooms. Her research has been published in journals including *American Educational Research Journal, College Composition and Communication, Educational Researcher, Linguistics and Education, Teachers College Record, Teaching and Teacher Education, and Written Communication.* Mary is also the author of a book, *The Rhetoric of Teaching: Understanding the Dynamics of Holocaust Narratives in an English Classroom* (2009, Hampton). She received a 2005 Promising Researcher Award from the National Council of Teachers of English. More information about her work can be found at www.msu.edu/~mmjuzwik.

*Stephanie L. Kerschbaum* is an Assistant Professor of English at the University of Delaware. Her research program uses rhetorical and linguistic methods to document how differences are understood and engaged within a variety of institutional contexts. She is particularly interested in the intersections between cultural and institutional rhetorics of diversity and individual identity as it is shaped in and around practices of writing.

*Lesley Ann Rex* is Professor Emerita and former co-chair of the Joint PhD Program in English and Education at the University of Michigan, Ann Arbor. She is interested in English language arts literacy education at the secondary level and in ethnographic and discourse analytic research that promotes equitable, meaningful and productive teaching and learning. Both interests converge in her books *Discourse of Opportunity: How Talk in Learning Situations Creates and Constrains* (Hampton, 2006) and *Using Discourse Analysis to Improve Classroom Interaction* (Taylor & Francis, 2009, with Laura Schiller). Her expertise extends to research on classroom interaction (*Handbook of Complementary Methods for Research in Education,* AERA, 2006) and to discourse analytic studies in literacy (*Reading Research Quarterly,* 2010*).* Her own research has appeared in *Journal of Literacy Research, Reading Research Quarterly, Research in the Teaching of English, Teaching and Teacher Education, Linguistics and Education, Communication Education, American Educational Research Journal,* and *Teachers College Record.* Additional information can be found at http://www.umich.edu/~rex/.

*Betsy Rymes* is Associate Professor of Educational Linguistics in the Graduate School of Education at the University of Pennsylvania. Her research, theoretically and methodologically informed by linguistic anthropology, is centered on educational contexts and examines how languages, social interaction, and institutions influence an individual's educational and social trajectory. Her research has been published in a range of journals, including *Harvard Educational Review, Language in Society,*

*Linguistics & Education, TESOL Quarterly,* and *Discourse & Society.* She is the author of two books, *Conversational Borderlands: Language and Identity in an Alternative Urban High School* (2001, Teachers College) and *Classroom Discourse Analysis: A Tool for Critical Reflection* (2009, Hampton).

**Stanton Wortham** is the Judy and Howard Berkowitz Professor and Associate Dean for Academic Affairs at the University of Pennsylvania Graduate School of Education. His research applies techniques from linguistic anthropology to study interactional positioning and social identity development in classrooms. He is particularly interested in interrelations between the official curriculum and covert interactional patterns in classroom discourse, and in how the processes of learning and identity development interconnect. His publications include *Narratives in Action* (Teachers College Press, 2001), *Education in the New Latino Diaspora* (Ablex, 2002; coedited with Enrique Murillo and Edmund Hamann), *Linguistic Anthropology of Education* (Praeger, 2003, coedited with Betsy Rymes), *Learning Identity* (Cambridge, 2006), and *Bullish on Uncertainty* (Cambridge, 2009, with Alexandra Michel). More information about his work can be found at http://www.gse.upenn.edu/~stantonw.

**Andrea Zellner** is a former high school English teacher at Southfield-Lathrup High School in Southfield, Michigan, where she taught 9th-, 10th-, and 11th-grade Composition and Literature and Honors Composition and Literature. She became a Red Cedar Writing Project (RCWP) Teacher Consultant in 2005 and is currently working for RCWP at Michigan State University.

# AUTHOR INDEX

# SUBJECT INDEX

CPSIA information can be obtained at www.ICGtesting.com
Printed in the USA
267737BV00010B/1/P